Modes of Writing
ARGUMENTS

For Hilary and Jackie

Modes of Writing

ARGUMENTS

Stephen Clarke and John Sinker

Series editor: Richard Andrews

CAMBRIDGE
UNIVERSITY PRESS

Published by the Press Syndicate of the University of Cambridge
The Pitt Building, Trumpington Street, Cambridge CB2 IRP
40 West 20th Street, New York, NY 10011-4211, USA
10 Stamford Road, Oakleigh, Victoria 3166, Australia

© Cambridge University Press 1992

First published 1992

Printed in Great Britain by Scotprint Ltd, Musselburgh

A catalogue record for this book is available from the British Library

ISBN 0 521 39989 0 paperback

Produced by Zoë Books Limited
15, Worthy Lane, Winchester,
Hampshire SO23 7AB

Designed by Sterling Associates
Artwork by Linda Combi
Picture Research by Valerie Randall

Cover design by Linda Combi

MODES OF WRITING

Modes of Writing is a series which aims to bring a wide range of writing to the attention of students aged fourteen and upwards. It consists of three anthologies: *Narratives, Arguments and Descriptions.*

Narratives is a collection of stories, anecdotes, tales, comic strips, myths, fables and letters, all of which depend on the linking of events and states of mind in a sequence. The sequence takes place in time, though the 'events' may not necessarily be told in chronological order. Indeed, one of the points of this collection is to show that playing with time rather than simply representing time in writing is what narrative enables us to do. Another of the intentions here is to make it clear that narrative can be used not only to tell one's own story (as in autobiography), or in fiction, but also to record scientific observations, to argue a case (as in fables) and as a way of thinking.

Arguments includes everything from a letter by Groucho Marx to a letter from a parent to a headteacher about school uniform; from cartoons to travel writing; from poems to a Monty Python script. Here it is the putting over of a point of view that is the focus rather than the telling of a sequence of events. The interrelationship of ideas is of more interest than the relationship with time. People are using language to persuade others to adopt their point of view, and they are using language in a much more varied way than the conventional 'essay' suggests (or allows).

The third book in the series, *Descriptions*, covers the range of writing which attempts to stay close to things in the world. Sometimes it uses narrative (as in reports), and at other times it argues a point simply through describing what it sees. On further occasions - in commentary, in conveying its subject matter in the present tense - it depends on neither of these methods, but appears to have a life of its own. It moves easily backwards and forwards between the 'real world' and the worlds of fiction (though it also sees the real world as one of a number of possible worlds).

If there appears to be a degree of overlap between these three books, that is part of the plan. These are not watertight categories with their own rules, but ways of organising writing which are flexible and which can be combined. Part of the aim of the series is to encourage invention, risk-taking and cross-over between these modes of composition, in 'English' and in other subjects.

By building the series on the principle of broad modes of writing rather than by themes or authors, we also draw attention to the different types of language that are available to writers as they compose. This is a series *about* language as well as one which is promoting the use of language in lively, productive and entertaining ways.

Lastly, we have wanted to produce books that are arguments in themselves: books which present a certain vision of the possibilities in language, but which are also there to argue with. To this end, we have tried to demystify the process of compiling the anthologies. We have demonstrated the thinking that has led to a particular choice of text or to a particular sequencing of texts. We hope that you will use these books critically: enter into a dialogue with the texts and go beyond the suggestions we have made in the activities.

Richard Andrews

CONTENTS

INTRODUCTION

We have often felt puzzled by text books. For a start, books *are* texts, they are also, self-evidently, books. Puzzling! *Buddy* or *Sumitra's Story* are texts; they are also books. But they're not text books. Even stranger is that many 'text books' have a weird introduction (this introduction you might find pretty weird but that's not what we have in mind.) Firstly there's usually a page or two addressed 'to the teacher', then, typically, half a page 'to the pupil'. So who is the rest of the book for? Why has it been written? For what kind of person? What will you gain by more or less dutifully wading through all the exercises and activities? Does the writer ever tell you? Is the writing from God? If there is a real person at the other end talking to you, why doesn't she or he let you know?

Be on your guard, don't talk to strange text book writers.

Activity
In groups if you want
● Decide on six books which you have come across which you think are text books. Decide why they are - what features they have in common. (It helps to have some in front of you; most schools and colleges have quite a few old ones lying around!)
● Can you tell *anything* about the writer and about her/his motives?
● Create a fantasy figure for one of your authors. Did the book lead to instant fame or is the writer now languishing in jail?

Psst! Didn't our introduction say something about text books tending not to tell you *why* you were doing things? And about strange people talking to you?

Some books, but not this one, have a picture of the author(s) and brief biographical information on the cover. The picture is usually a serious portrait (why?). We'll spare you the biography but opposite is a picture of one of us.

Of course we've cheated since this picture is thirty seven years old. Let one of us, John Sinker, explain:

"My brother (the babe in arms) is now huge and used to play American football. Sadly Mum and Dad have died. I'm the six-year-old facing the firing squad in a brand new unbendable jacket. But at least it's serious."

Activity
● Get together a small collection of photographs of yourself. If you have access to a camera take shots of your friends.

● Decide which pictures would best suit the book that you might one day write. Is our picture the sort you would use? Why not?

● Look at the pictures of your friends. How far does the background of the picture influence you? (A boy one of us knew a long time ago sent his school - for its office records - a picture of him, aged 12¼, leaning on his dad's pink Rolls Royce.)

● Does what you wear affect what others might think? What do you *want* your unknown readers to think?

This, then, is a personal introduction which has told you some biographical details about one of us - John Sinker. You may also infer certain things from the language used. Argument is never neutral, it is always within a context of language and biography, however 'impersonal' the issue being addressed.

This is a book about argument, about hearing ideas, agreeing, savouring or refuting them. In a sense it's a book about arguing back, saying no, asking: 'Does it have to be this way?' It's a book about making passionate assertions of agreement or statements of qualified support, statements of doubt or requests for evidence.

This introduction is itself a sort of argument; we are trying to persuade you of certain propositions, not least that the world is teeming and brimming with argument and debate which are the property of us all. We hope you will find much in this selection that makes you want to argue back - in writing, in speaking to others or simply in thinking.

We have no wish to tell you how to use this book. Our ideas are now in your hands and become your property to shape into your ideas. We, as editors, have chosen pieces which strike us as worthwhile and interesting and we have ordered our material in a particular way. You may well wish to challenge both the ordering and the selection. We hope you will.

Arguments can sometimes change the world.

Stephen Clarke and John Sinker

PROTEST

Introduction

Arguments can be about almost anything and can originate in any number of relationships, from close to formal. Most argument is spoken, but some is also printed. To argue does not necessarily signify that anything is wrong in the world or that the relationship is a negative one - quite the contrary. We are probably mentally healthier for arguing things out, for discovering that ideas don't just lie around like stones, but are brought to life by debate and reason and the passionate use of evidence, even if 'evidence' means telling what happened to you that time when ...

'Protest' isn't quite like that. To protest about something does suggest that there is a wrong in the world that needs putting right; an injustice that must be pointed out or argued against, and perhaps in public. However, how you right wrongs or protest against things or people, even just by writing, is not an activity to which strict rules apply. You can be funny or bitingly sarcastic or sad rather than angry. You can pretend to be someone other than yourself as you write and thus you can say things that are preposterous because they don't appear to be your own personal ideas. This is what Swift does, for example, in the passage entitled *A Modest Proposal*. It isn't modest at all to propose to eat babies, nor does Swift believe that, but he needs to find a way of voicing his protest against the hunger and poverty that he finds around him. Somehow he has to reach an audience and shock them, but not by a display of anger, for those who seem calm are probably listened to more attentively than angry people, especially at first. Other writers in this section do not seek to shock; they protest by reasoning or by making us laugh at the perpetrators of wrong.

Powerful protest can change things, can make a difference to the world. How you choose to protest may depend upon what it is that you are protesting about. For instance, school uniform is not as serious a matter as the slaughter of species, classroom violence or racist arrogance, and so protest about it can be handled differently from these other subjects in style and tone. The pieces in this section have in common a sense of sincere protest and a sense, too, that the writers are concerned about others - they are not just wingeing on their own behalf.

Activity
- Arrange the pieces in this section into three groups. They could be grouped by style, by content or by quality (the best pieces, the middling ones and the worst).

Back to School

'Back to School' is an extract from the book *Attacks of Opinion*, a collection of pieces written for younger readers of *The Guardian* newspaper by Terry Jones, who was one of the Monty Python team.

Well it's the start of a new school term, and once again I find myself worrying about just what is going on in our schools. Is Maggie doing enough to 'protect children from being brain-washed and to keep political indoctrination out of the playground', as she promised she would?

Some teachers, I believe, are still openly giving lessons on the Peasants' Revolt of 1381 and the history of the trade union movement in the nineteenth century as if both were somehow explained by the social conditions of the day! What's more, I understand that in many schools, teachers still talk about the Second World War as if it had been fought against a Fascist dictatorship rather than the creeping menace of international communism!

Of course, all of us are grateful for the 1986 Education Act which, thanks to Baroness Cox and her campaign to take politics out of the classroom, made it illegal to teach partisan political views in schools. But it is now clear that the Act did not go nearly far enough.

You see it is all too easy for political bias to creep in, even when the views being expressed are apparently harmless. The chemistry teacher's tone of voice, for example, as he describes Mrs Thatcher's achievements in that field, could all too easily convey disrespect or even ridicule. Similarly, a raised eyebrow or a sideways smirk, as the Religious Instruction teacher spells out the dangers of liberalism in the Church of England, could actually undermine the return to traditional values that the Revd Gummer has demanded.

Once a leftie always a leftie is what I say, and no amount of legislation is going to ensure political balance in such a teacher's classroom.

It seems to me that the only way finally to eradicate politics from the classroom is to vet all teachers for left-wing sympathies. Political activists should be rooted out at the training stage. And though this may mean losing some of the best trainee teachers, extra points could be awarded to the politically apathetic to ensure that enough qualify, and to make up for any intellectual shortcomings or lack of teaching ability in otherwise suitable candidates. Far better to have dull or even uninspiring instructors for our young, than ones with a political axe to grind.

And should any deviants slip through the net, and start sowing the seeds of socialism in our schools, why not encourage pupils to report on any teacher who steps out of line? They could do so anonymously, either to the head-master or else to some regulatory body approved by Conservative central office, and the offender could be booted out before he can guess where his next pay-packet is coming from.

The Prime Minister has declared her ambition to eradicate

socialism from these shores by the end of her term in office. So far she and Mr Kinnock have succeeded in eliminating it only from politics. If the good work is going to continue surely it is essential to banish all closet lefties from the classroom (pupils as well as teachers), to suppress all discussion of liberal ideas in schools, and to rid the library shelves once and for all of the works of all subversives like: Karl Marx, Keir Hardie, William Godwin, Robert Owen, William Cobbett, Charles Dickens, H. G. Wells, George Bernard Shaw, Oscar Wilde, Mrs Gaskell, William Blake, Wordsworth, Milton, Burns, Swift, Byron, Shelley and Christ.

Terry Jones
13 January 1988

Activities
- Write a spoof letter about 'lefties' to the Conservative Party Central Office. (You may also like to consider doing the same about right-wingers to the Labour Party.)
- Humour and exaggeration are here being used to achieve emphasis. Defend your own political or social beliefs by using a similar method.
- In groups, work up an improvisation where a right-wing member of staff complains 'in the strongest possible terms' to the Head or principal

about a young 'leftie' who has just joined the staff. Go for a Pythonesque piece of comic exaggeration. You may like to reverse this and produce a satiric view of a left-winger's prejudices.

This Earth is Precious

Chief Seattle's reply has become well known as a poster, a T-shirt and a postcard. But for all of that he strikes us as worth studying. Here is a piece of writing coming, in 1845, from a culture that was considered barbaric by the Washington government of the white invaders of America.

How can you buy or sell the sky, the warmth of the land? The idea is strange to us.

If we do not own the freshness of the air and the sparkle of the water, how can you buy them?

Every part of this earth is sacred to my people.

Every shining pine needle, every sandy shore, every mist in the dark woods, every clearing and humming insect is holy in the memory and experience of my people. The sap which courses through the trees carries the memories of the red man.

The white man's dead forget the country of their birth when they go to walk among the stars. Our dead never forget this beautiful earth, for it is the mother of the red man.

We are part of the earth and it is part of us.

The perfumed flowers are our sisters; the deer, the horse, the great eagle, these are our brothers.

The rocky crests, the juices in the meadows, the body heat of the pony, and man - all belong to the same family.

So, when the Great Chief in Washington sends word that he wishes to buy our land, he asks much of us. The Great Chief sends word he will reserve us a place so that we can live comfortably to ourselves.

He will be our father and we will be his children. So we will consider your offer to buy our land.

But it will not be easy. For this land is sacred to us.

This shining water that moves in the streams and rivers is not just water but the blood of our ancestors.

If we sell you land, you must remember that it is sacred, and you must teach your children that it is sacred and that each ghostly reflection in the clear water of the lakes tells of events and memories in the life of my people.

The water's murmur is the voice of my father's father.

The rivers are our brothers, they quench our thirst. The rivers carry our canoes, and feed our children. If we sell you our land, you must remember, and teach your children, that the rivers are our brothers, and yours, and you must henceforth give the rivers the kindness you would give any brother.

We know that the white man does not understand our ways. One portion of land is the same to him as the next, for he is a stranger who comes in the night and takes from the land whatever he needs.

The earth is not his brother, but his enemy, and when he has conquered it, he moves on.

He leaves his father's graves behind, and he does not care. He kidnaps the earth from his children, and he does not care.

His father's grave, and his children's birthright, are forgotten. He treats his mother, the earth, and his brother, the sky, as things to be bought, plundered, sold like sheep or bright beads.

His appetite will devour the earth and leave behind only a desert.

I do not know. Our ways are different from your ways.

The sight of your cities pains the eyes of the red man. But perhaps it is because the red man is a savage and does not understand.

There is no quiet place in the white man's cities. No place to hear the unfurling of leaves in spring, or the rustle of an insect's wings.

But perhaps it is because I am a savage and do not understand.

The clatter only seems to insult the ears. And what is there to life if a man cannot hear the lonely cry of the whippoorwill or the arguments of the frogs around a pond at night? I am a red man and do not understand.

The Indian prefers the soft sound of the wind darting over the face of a pond, and the smell of the wind itself, cleaned by a midday rain, or scented with the pinon pine.

The air is precious to the red man, for all things share the same breath - the beast, the tree, the man, they all share the same breath.

The white man does not seem to notice the air he breathes. Like a man dying for many days, he is numb to the stench.

But if we sell you our land, you must remember that the air is precious to us, that the air shares its spirit with all the life it supports. The wind that gave our grandfather his first breath also receives his last sigh.

And if we sell you our land, you must keep it apart and sacred, as a place where even the white man can go to taste the wind that is sweetened by the meadow's flowers.

So we will consider your offer to buy our land. If we decide to accept, I will make one condition: The white man must treat the beasts of this land as his brothers.

I am a savage and I do not understand any other way.

I have seen a thousand rotting buffaloes on the prairie, left by the white man who shot them from a passing train.

I am a savage and I do not understand how the smoking iron horse can be more important than the buffalo that we kill only to stay alive.

What is man without the beasts? If all the beasts were gone, man would die from a great loneliness of spirit.

For whatever happens to the beasts, soon happens to man. All things are connected.

You must teach your children that the ground beneath their feet is the ashes of your grandfathers. So that they will respect the land, tell your children that the earth is rich with the lives of our kin.

Teach your children what we have taught our children, that the earth is our mother.

Whatever befalls the earth befalls the sons of the earth. If men spit upon the ground, they spit upon themselves.

This we know: The earth does not belong to man; man belongs to the earth. This we know.

All things are connected like the blood which unites one family. All things are connected.

Whatever befalls the earth befalls the sons of the earth. Man did not weave the web of life: he is merely a strand in it. Whatever he does to the web, he does to himself.

Even the white man, whose God walks and talks with him as friend to friend, cannot be exempt from the common destiny.

We may be brothers after all.

We shall see.

One thing we know, which the white man may one day discover - our God is the same God.

You may think now that you own Him as you wish to own our land; but you cannot. He is the God of man, and His compassion is equal for the red man and the white.

This earth is precious to Him, and to harm the earth is to heap contempt on its Creator.

The whites too shall pass; perhaps sooner than all other tribes. Contaminate your bed, and you will one night suffocate in your own waste.

But in your perishing you will shine brightly, fired by the strength of the God who brought you to this land and for some special purpose gave you dominion over this land and over the red man.

That destiny is a mystery to us, for we do not understand when the buffalo are all slaughtered, the wild horses are tamed, the secret corners of the forest heavy with scent of many men, and the view of the ripe hills blotted by talking wires.

Where is the thicket? Gone.
Where is the eagle? Gone.
The end of living and the beginning of survival.

Chief Seattle
1845

Activities

● Discuss how Chief Seattle composed his argument. Try to write a paragraph in his style in which you defend your home environment against a realistic modern threat, e.g. a nuclear dump, an airport, a motorway.

● Role-play: re-read the text, making notes on the main points or argument. Enact the meeting of the chief and his advisers with the President in Washington and his advisers. Can a solution be found to the threat posed to Chief Seattle's people?

● Research: present a report for the group on similar threats being posed to indigenous populations today. (You might know something about Sting's work with people in the Brazilian rain forest.)

● Is Western civilisation all a mistake? Write a counter-argument in defence of Western civilisation.

Arguments about Architecture

Jackie Witkin

Jackie Witkin

Activities
- Look at the pictures and decide:
1 Which ones are ugly, if any.
2 Which ones look as if the community cared about them.
3 Which ones you would be prepared to spend money on were they to start to crumble.
4 Which ones are best knocked down to make way for something better.

Leningrad

Gavin Stamp is a travel writer. What strikes us about his writing here is
the passion behind it - the sense that British post-war building was so
ugly, so uncaring about the past and the achievements of those who
built our great cities.

Behind the old barracks of Tsarskoe Selo, way off the Intourist track,
we found what we were looking for: a ruined Neo-Classical Church,
four-square with four Greek Doric porticoes and a low dome,
standing forlorn in a muddy expanse of waste ground. A shabbily
dressed native, picking through the rubbish, came up to us; amongst
an incomprehensible stream of Russian we recognised one word -
Kameron - which is to say Charles Cameron, the British architect
imported along with other Western artists by Catherine the Great.
The equivalent in Britain is hard to imagine with any conviction: a
tramp outside, say, the Lyceum in Liverpool - "tis by Thomas
'arrison, sir. Can yer spare the price of a cup of tea ..."

In Britain, war-damaged buildings seldom survived long as ruins;
the sites were too valuable, the planners too eager. Thirty years after
the Blitz, the proud shell of Wren's Christ Church, Newgate Street,
suffered the indignity of being half demolished for a road. But it is
typical of Russia that the cathedral of St Sophia, battle-scarred and
crumbling, still stands awaiting restoration and, when the builders
and craftsmen have finished the remaining rooms in Rastrelli's
Baroque palace and completed the rebuilding of Cameron's Chinese
village, doubtless they will turn their attention to his church.

The remarkable restorations of the palaces of the Tsars by the
Russians are rightly famous. Peterhof, Tsarskoe Selo and Pavlovsk
were all left smashed and gutted after the Germans retreated from
Leningrad in 1944. Repairs began almost immediately and still
continue. Original drawings and documents were acquired and
studied; craftsmen sent to Italy to be trained. The result is a series of
magnificent, scholarly and costly re-creations of rooms which make
the care of country houses by our own National Trust seem amateur.

All this is well known; the great surprise of a visit to Leningrad is
that the whole centre of the city is intact and beautifully preserved.
Yet from September 1941, Leningrad was besieged by the Germans
for almost 900 days; a million died - over half from starvation - and
the city was constantly bombed and shelled. Apart from memorials
and appalling mass cemeteries, there is nothing to show for this
today. The streets are intact, the public buildings and palaces all
extant. Not a single modern building breaks the delicate skyline and
dares challenge the dome of St Isaac's Cathedral or the gilded spires

St Isaac's Cathedral

of the Admiralty and the Peter and Paul Fortress. A comparison with London - a city which suffered less and where very few of the Wren City churches have been really well restored - is inevitable and, for an English visitor, painful.

The citizens of Leningrad evidently care deeply about their buildings - as well they might. Although the first buildings raised by Peter the Great after the foundation of the city in 1703 and by his daughter Elizabeth are Baroque, the real character of St Petersburg-Petrograd-Leningrad was created between the reigns of Catherine and her grandson Nicholas I - 1762 to 1856 - and it is now quite simply the finest Neo-Classical city in the world. Western architects - Cameron, the Italians Rossi and Quarenghi, the Frenchman de Thomon - brought a new style to the banks of the Neva which took root and was then developed with native brilliance by Russian architects - Zacharov, Voronikhin, Stasov. That a style which emulated the severe purity of the Antique, sharply modelled in the Mediterranean sun, should have flourished so healthily in the cold north of Europe is a strange paradox, but Edinburgh, Berlin, Helsinki and St Petersburg still stand to show that Neo-Classicism was more concerned with republican or revolutionary ideals (even *pace* Washington).

Much of Berlin remains in ruins, but in 1945 Leningrad was evidently determined to recreate the beauty of the city and its palaces. The fact that it was built by and for the Tsars did not worry them - the buildings were made by (on the whole) Russian craftsmen and belonged to the Russian people, and it is touching to find at Pavlovsk a room devoted to the architects, painters and craftsmen who have restored the palace since the war. This is an attitude to the national heritage which contrasts markedly with that manifested by city authorities in Britain since 1945, both Labour and Conservative. Councils in Newcastle, Manchester and elsewhere seemed determined to remove all trace of the wicked capitalist past - but there was one Socialist politician who should be remembered with honour: Attlee, who used his casting vote in Cabinet to save the war-worn Nash terraces in Regent's Park (whereas Macmillan, ostensibly a Conservative, personally permitted the Euston Arch and the Clarendon Hotel, Oxford, to be demolished).

Perhaps we are too old a nation, perhaps we have been too confident and complacent, to need to keep our historic buildings and cities as visible expressions and symbols of national identity - but we have certainly recognised that necessity in others. 'Bomber' Harris struck a blow at German cultural pride when he ordered the RAF to destroy the old mediaeval Hanseatic cities of Lübeck and Rostock in 1941. The Germans, furious, swiftly retaliated with the 'Baedeker' raids, but the city authorities of Exeter, Canterbury and elsewhere did not try to recreate their scarred cities after the war. Instead, architects and planners almost welcomed the Blitz as an opportunity for modernisation and many damaged buildings which could have been repaired were pulled down. Even worse, of course, has sometimes been the fate of those historic towns which did not enjoy the attentions of the Luftwaffe: foreign tourists often assume today that the horrible redevelopments in, say Worcester and Gloucester are the result of bombing, when they are nothing of the kind.

Not that the Russians are incapable of calculated vandalism: pride in national monuments can work in reverse. In the march into Germany, the Soviet armies destroyed Königsberg, the birthplace of Kant and the ancient capital of East Prussia, expelled its German population and renamed it Kaliningrad. Similarly, since 1945 a policy of cultural imperialism has been pursued in the Islamic parts of the Soviet Empire, where the narrow streets, bazaars and mosques of old Muslim cities have been replaced by modern Western-style redevelopments in a deliberate attempt to undermine a culture by destroying its context. Nor should the large number of churches and other old buildings destroyed by Stalin in Moscow be forgotten.

The centre of Leningrad nevertheless remains a dream. The oppressiveness and sheer awfulness of Soviet Communism is still there to be seen and felt, of course; the queues, the absence of any pleasant places to eat or drink, the slogans. It seemed most like *1984* on the day of unpaid labour, the *corvée* in honour of Lenin, when 'Music While You Work' blared from loudspeakers all over the city and even in the gardens at Pavlovsk. But, to the Western visitor, there can be compensations in addition to the completeness of the architecture: few cars and a cheap, efficient public transport, the absence of advertisements (apart from the absurd ikons of Communist saints) and of offensive pornography.

Although it was not Communism which has made the Czechs preserve the unspoiled beauty of Prague, which inspired the Poles to reconstruct Warsaw and Danzig as they were, and which moved the women of Dresden to start repairing the Zwinger within weeks of the fire-bomb attack, it is true that the dampening effect of Soviet rule has saved Eastern Europe from many of the mistakes of the West. If the Iron Curtain ever lifts, Europe will still be divided in two physically; in the one half historic cities rebuilt and preserved, in the other cities ruined by a combination of foolish utopianism and sheer greed.

The great beauty of Leningrad, an authoritarian city built largely with forced labour, can be profoundly disturbing for a British visitor, for it highlights a strange paradox: that Soviet Russia, officially wedded to a determinist, progressive view of history, is in fact very conservative and preserves its Tsarist past at great expense; while, in theoretically free and individualistic Britain, where any intelligent sensitive person is acutely conscious of cultural decline, intellectuals have for decades felt that tradition must surrender to the supposed demands of a dominating idea of progress - in architecture as in other spheres. Just look at modern Bath.

Gavin Stamp
16 May 1981

Paradox
At the heart of this piece lies a paradox. Paradox is an inherent contradiction: here is a society, Russia, that was authoritarian and communist and yet has apparently shown a greater respect for its historic tradition of building than we have in the West.

Activities
● Imagine you arrived in New York or London or any other large city in the 'developed' world from a poor, rural background in Africa or Asia (a kind of super-aware Crocodile Dundee). Think of all the experiences you could have which would, in a letter home, suggest that 'developed' people were a good deal less civilised and clever than 'undeveloped' people. For example, how would road systems, fast food outlets and high rise dwellings strike anyone with a more humane view of the world? You may like to write this in the form of a poem.
● Beg or borrow a camera. Take, in groups, a folio of pictures to illustrate good and bad architecture in your locality. Be prepared to justify your decisions and try to establish your group's criteria.

Bleak House

Charles Dickens wrote in great anger against what he saw as some of the injustices of Victorian England, including the legal system.

LONDON. Michaelmas Term lately over, and the Lord Chancellor sitting in Lincoln's Inn Hall. Implacable November weather. As much mud in the streets, as if the waters had but newly retired from the face of the earth, and it would not be wonderful to meet a Megalosaurus, forty feet long or so, waddling like an elephantine lizard up Holborn Hill. Smoke lowering down from chimney-pots, making a soft black drizzle, with flakes of soot in it as big as full-grown snow-flakes - gone into mourning, one might imagine, for the death of the sun. Dogs, undistinguishable in mire. Horses, scarcely better; splashed to their very blinkers. Foot passengers, jostling one another's umbrellas, in a general infection of ill-temper, and losing their foot-hold at street-corners, where tens of thousands of other foot passengers have been slipping and sliding since the day broke (if this day ever broke), adding new deposits to the crust upon crust of mud, sticking at those points tenaciously to the pavement, and accumulating at compound interest.

Fog everywhere. Fog up the river, where it flows among green aits and meadows; fog down the river, where it rolls defiled among the tiers of shipping, and the waterside pollutions of a great (and dirty) city. Fog on the Essex marshes, fog on the Kentish heights. Fog creeping into the cabooses of collier-brigs, fog lying out on the yards, and hovering in the rigging of great ships; fog drooping on the gunwales of barges and small boats. Fog in the eyes and throats of ancient Greenwich pensioners, wheezing by the firesides of their wards; fog in the stem and bowl of the afternoon pipe of the wrathful skipper, down in his close cabin; fog cruelly pinching the toes and fingers of his shivering little 'prentice boy on deck. Chance people on the bridges peeping over the parapets into a nether sky of fog, with fog all round them, as if they were up in a balloon, and hanging in the misty clouds.

Gas looming through the fog in divers places in the streets, much as the sun may, from the spongy fields, be seen to loom by husbandman and ploughboy. Most of the shops lighted two hours before their time - as the gas seems to know, for it has a haggard and unwilling look.

The raw afternoon is rawest, and the dense forest is densest, and the muddy streets are muddiest, near that leaden-headed old obstruction, appropriate ornament for the threshold of a leaden-headed old corporation: Temple Bar. And hard by Temple Bar, in Lincoln's Inn Hall, at the very heart of the fog, sits the Lord High Chancellor in his High Court of Chancery.

Never can there come fog too thick, never can there come mud and mire too deep, to assort with the groping and floundering condition which this High Court of Chancery, most pestilent of hoary sinners, holds, this day, in the sight of heaven and earth.

On such an afternoon, if ever, the Lord High Chancellor ought to be sitting here - as here he is - with a foggy glory round his head, softly fenced in with crimson cloth and curtains, addressed by a large advocate with great whiskers, a little voice, and an interminable brief, and outwardly directing his contemplation to the lantern in the roof, where he can see nothing but fog. On such an afternoon, some score of members of the High Court of Chancery bar ought to be - as here they are - mistily engaged in one of the ten thousand stages of an endless cause, tripping one another up on slippery precedents, groping knee-deep in technicalities, running their goat-hair and horse-hair warded heads against walls of words, and making a pretence of equity with serious faces, as players might. On such an afternoon, the various solicitors in the cause, some two or three of whom have inherited it from their fathers, who made a fortune by it, ought to be - as are they not? - ranged in a line, in a long matted well (but you might look in vain for Truth at the bottom of it), between the registrar's red table and the silk gowns, with bills, cross-bills, answers, rejoinders, injunctions, affidavits, issues, references to masters, masters' reports, mountains of costly nonsense, piled before them. Well may the court be dim, with wasting candles here and there; well may the fog hang heavy in it, as if it would never get out; well may the stained glass windows lose their colour, and admit no light of day into the place; well may the uninitiated from the streets, who peep in through the glass panes in the door, be deterred from entrance by its owlish aspect, and by the drawl languidly echoing to the roof from the padded dais where the Lord High Chancellor looks into the lantern that has no light in it, and where the attendant wigs are all stuck in a fog bank! This is the Court of Chancery; which has its decaying houses and its blighted lands in every shire; which has its worn-out lunatic in every madhouse, and its dead in every churchyard; which has its ruined suitor, with his slipshod heels and threadbare dress, borrowing and begging through the round of every man's acquaintance; which gives to monied might, the means abundantly of wearing out the right; which so exhausts finances, patience, courage, hope; so overthrows the brain and breaks the heart; that there is not an honourable man among its practitioners who would not give - who does not often give - the warning, 'Suffer any wrong that can be done you, rather than come here!'

Charles Dickens

Activities

● In groups of three or four, write a list of five questions that you would like to ask about this text.

● Turn this passage into the words of a song (if you can perform it, so much the better).

● You might wonder why this piece is here since it is clearly a description. However, what Dickens is doing is using fog as a metaphor for his attack on the legal profession and its endless inability to see anything clearly except its own profit.

Try your hand at describing something so that you are also showing your attitude towards the person or object or idea in mind.

● Read as much as you can of another Dickens novel. We recommend: *Great Expectations*, *Oliver Twist*, *Hard Times*. (There are also some excellent, if a little dated, films of some of Dickens' novels. We particularly like the somewhat antique version of *David Copperfield* which has the wonderful W.C. Fields as Wilkins Micawber.)

● Notice the language. Not one main verb in the first three paragraphs! What is a sentence, anyway? What effect is Dickens achieving by breaking the 'rules'?

Letter to School

Brian Tuffin was once a schoolteacher; he also possesses a delightful sense of humour.

```
Dear Mr Rhodes,

As a newly-acting parent I have been looking forward
to my first letter from the School. I am not
disappointed.
    I would just like to check that I have
interpreted the uniform rules correctly.
    Assuming I have two children I must send one in
a tie, but not the other. One can wear an ear stud
but the other must not. Normally, one must wear
trousers of a certain colour but the other must not
wear trousers unless it is cold, in which case it is
permissible to wear them but not in the same colour.
One must have black or brown shoes (with grey
trousers) but the other could have pink or green
shoes or even wellingtons as long as they don't have
sharp heels. If the weather changes then these rules
also change.
    It seems that if the weather is variable and if
boys and girls choose to wear their hair in a
variety of lengths you will be hard pressed to
choose who to send home. I wish you the best of
luck.

Yours with a smile,
Brian Tuffin
```

Activities
● Write the Deputy Headteacher's reply.
● School uniform in Britain is still a live issue. Interview fellow students about their view on uniform. Make a tape of varied voices and opinions.
● If you think there should be some kind of rules concerning physical appearance at school, write them down in a way which will avoid misinterpretation.

Running Battle with Warner Brothers

Groucho Marx probably needs little introduction. He was one of the great comic actors and writers in films in the 1930s and 1940s, along with his brothers, Chico, Harpo and (in some of the films) Zeppo. We include his letter here as an example of how effective protest can be comical and irreverent rather than serious.

When the Marx Brothers were about to make a movie called 'A Night in Casablanca,' there were threats of legal action from the Warner Brothers, who, five years before, had made a film called, simply, 'Casablanca' (with Humphrey Bogart and Ingrid Bergman as stars). Whereupon Groucho, speaking for his brothers and himself, immediately dispatched the following letters:

Dear Warner Brothers:

Apparently there is more than one way of conquering a city and holding it as your own. For example, up to the time that we contemplated making this picture, I had no idea that the city of Casablanca belonged exclusively to Warner Brothers. However, it was only a few days after our announcement appeared that we received your long, ominous legal document warning us not to use the name Casablanca.

It seems that in 1471, Ferdinand Balboa Warner, your great great-grandfather, while looking for a shortcut to the city of Burbank, had stumbled on the shores of Africa and, raising his alpenstock (which he later turned in for a hundred shares of the common), named it Casablanca.

I just don't understand your attitude. Even if you plan on re-releasing your picture, I am sure that the average movie fan could learn in time to distinguish between Ingrid Bergman and Harpo. I don't know whether I could, but I certainly would like to try.

You claim you own Casablanca and that no one else can use that name without your permission. What about 'Warner Brothers'? Do you own that, too? You probably have the right to use the name Warner, but what about Brothers? Professionally, we were brothers long before you were. We were touring the sticks as The Marx Brothers when Vitaphone was still a gleam in the inventor's eye, and even before us there had been other brothers - the Smith Brothers; the Brothers Karamazov; Dan Brothers, an outfielder with Detroit; and 'Brother, Can You Spare a Dime?' (This was originally 'Brothers, Can You Spare a Dime?' but this was spreading a dime pretty thin, so they threw out one brother gave all the money to the other one and whittled it down to, 'Brother, Can You Spare a Dime?')

Now Jack, how about you? Do you maintain that yours is an original name? Well, it's not. It was used long before you were born. Offhand, I can think of two Jacks - there was Jack of 'Jack and the Beanstalk,' and Jack the Ripper, who cut quite a figure in his day.

As for you, Harry, you probably sign your checks, sure in the belief that you are the first Harry of all time and that all other Harrys are imposters. I can think of two Harrys that preceded you. There was Lighthouse Harry of Revolutionary fame and a Harry Appelbaum who lived on the corner of 93rd Street and Lexington Avenue. Unfortunately, Appelbaum wasn't too well known. The last I heard of him, he was selling neckties at Weber and Heilbroner.

Now about the Burbank studio. I believe this is what you brothers call your place. Old man Burbank is gone. Perhaps you remember him. He was a great man in a garden. His wife often said Luther had ten green thumbs. What a witty woman she must have been! Burbank was the wizard who crossed all those fruits and vegetables until he had the poor plants in such a confused and jittery condition that they could never decide whether to enter the dining room on the meat platter or the dessert dish.

This is pure conjecture, of course, but who knows - perhaps Burbank's survivors aren't too happy with the fact that a plant that grinds out pictures on a quota settled in their town, appropriated Burbank's name and uses it as a front for their films. It is even possible that the Burbank family is prouder of the potato produced by the old man than they are of the fact that from your studio emerged 'Casablanca' or even 'Gold Diggers of 1931'.

This all seems to add up to a pretty bitter tirade, but I assure you it's not meant to. I love Warners. Some of my best friends are Warner Brothers. It is even possible that I am doing you an injustice and that you, yourselves, know nothing at all about this dog-in-the-Wanger attitude. It wouldn't surprise me at all to discover that the heads of your legal department are unaware of this absurd dispute, for I am acquainted with many of them and they are fine fellows with curly black hair, double-breasted suits and a love of their fellow man that out-Saroyans Saroyan.

I have a hunch that this attempt to prevent us from using the title is the brainchild of some ferret-faced shyster, serving a brief apprenticeship in your legal department. I know the type well - hot out of law school, hungry for success and too ambitious to follow the natural laws of promotion. This bar sinister probably needled your attorneys, most of whom are fine fellows with curly black hair, double-breasted suits, etc., into attempting to enjoin us. Well, he won't get away with it! We'll fight him to the highest court! No pasty-faced legal adventurer is going to cause bad blood between the Warners and the Marxes. We are all brothers under the skin and we'll remain friends till the last reel of 'A Night in Casablanca' goes tumbling over the spool.

Sincerely,
Groucho Marx

For some curious reason, this letter seemed to puzzle the Warner Brothers legal department. They wrote - in all seriousness - and asked if the Marxes

could give them some idea of what their story was about. They felt that
something might be worked out. So Groucho replied:

Dear Warners:

There isn't much I can tell you about the story. In it I play a Doctor of
Divinity who ministers to the natives and, as a sideline, hawks can
openers and pea jackets to the savages along the Gold Coast of
Africa.

When I first meet Chico, he is working in a saloon, selling sponges
to barflies who are unable to carry their liquor. Harpo is an Arabian
caddie who lives in a small Grecian urn on the outskirts of the city.

As the picture opens, Porridge, a mealy-mouthed native girl, is
sharpening some arrows for the hunt. Paul Hangover, our hero, is
constantly lighting two cigarettes simultaneously. He apparently is
unaware of the cigarette shortage.

There are many scenes of splendor and fierce antagonisms, and
Color, an Abyssinian messenger boy, runs Riot. Riot, in case you
have never been there, is a small night club on the edge of town.

There's a lot more I could tell you, but I don't want to spoil it for
you. All this has been okayed by the Hays Office, Good
Housekeeping and the survivors of the Haymarket Riots; and if the
times are ripe, this picture can be the opening gun in a new
worldwide disaster.

> Cordially,
> Groucho Marx

Instead of mollifying them, this note seemed to puzzle the attorneys even
more; they wrote back and said they still didn't understand the story line
and they would appreciate it if Mr Marx would explain the plot in more
detail. So Groucho obliged with the following:

Dear Brothers:

Since I last wrote you, I regret to say there have been some changes
in the plot of our new picture, 'A Night in Casablanca.' In the new
version I play Bordello, the sweetheart of Humphrey Bogart. Harpo
and Chico are itinerant rug peddlers who are weary of laying rugs
and enter a monastery just for a lark. This is a good joke on them, as
there hasn't been a lark in the place for fifteen years.

Across from this monastery, hard by a jetty, is a waterfront hotel,
chockfull of apple-cheeked damsels, most of whom have been barred
by the Hays Office for soliciting. In the fifth reel, Gladstone makes a
speech that sets the House of Commons in a uproar and the King
promptly asks for his resignation. Harpo marries a hotel detective;

Chico operates an ostrich farm. Humphrey Bogart's girl, Bordello, spends her last years in a Bacall house.

This, as you can see, is a very skimpy outline. The only thing that can save us from extinction is a continuation of the film shortage.

Fondly,
Groucho Marx

After that, the Marxes heard no more from the Warner Brothers' legal department.

Activities
- Can you think of any reasons why Warner Brothers were anxious not to let the Marx Brothers use the idea of *Casablanca*?
- In groups, prepare a report on the work of the Marx Brothers; try to arrange a showing of some of their material.
- Try to watch *Casablanca*. Make a list (that you are prepared to defend in class) of ten movie classics.
- Copies of the original letters, from Warner Brothers, are not available to us as editors, but it's worth trying to imagine what they were like. Write the two letters that might have caused the last two replies from Groucho printed here, the ones ending 'cordially' and 'fondly'.

A Modest Proposal

Jonathan Swift (1677-1745) was Dean of the Anglican Cathedral in Dublin. He was an Irishman who wrote for a largely English audience, an audience that in the eighteenth century needed educating about Irish matters in general and the famine in particular. This cry for help from the people of Ireland came when three bad harvests in a row had caused particular hardship, but worse and more permanent was the deliberate economic oppression of the Irish by the English, who governed them.

A Modest Proposal was written (in 1729) as a bitter and sarcastic attack on British government policy. In our view it has yet to be surpassed in terms of its savage satire. A shortened version of the original is presented here.

It is a melancholly Object to those, who walk through this great Town,[1] or travel in the Country, when they see the *Streets*, the *Roads*, and *Cabbin-doors* crowded with *Beggars* of the Female Sex, followed

---

[1]   Dublin.

by three, four, or six Children, *all in Rags*, and importuning every Passenger for an Alms. These *Mothers*, instead of being able to work for their honest livelyhood, are forced to employ all their Time in stroling to beg Sustenance for their *helpless Infants*; who, as they grow up, either turn *Thieves* for want of Work; or leave their *dear Native Country, to fight for the Pretender in* Spain, or sell themselves to the *Barbadoes*.

I think it is agreed by all Parties, that this prodigious Number of Children in the Arms, or on the Backs, or at the *Heels* of their *Mothers*, and frequently of their *Fathers*, is *in the present deplorable State of the Kingdom*,[2] a very great additional Grievance; and therefore, whoever could find out a fair, cheap, and easy Method of making these Children sound and useful Members of the Commonwealth, would deserve so well of the Publick, as to have his Statue set up for a Preserver of the Nation.

But my Intention is very far from being confined to provide only for the Children of *professed Beggars*: It is of a much greater Extent, and shall take in the whole Number of Infants at a certain Age, who are born of Parents, in effect as little able to support them, as those who demand our Charity in the Streets ...

I shall now therefore humbly propose my own Thoughts; which I hope will not be liable to the least Objection.

I have been assured by a very knowing *American* of my Acquaintance in *London*; that a young healthy Child, well nursed, is, at a Year old, a most delicious, nourishing, and wholesome Food; whether *Stewed, Roasted, Baked,* or *Boiled*; and, I make no doubt, that it will equally serve in a *Fricasie*, or *Ragoust*.

I do therefore humbly offer it to *publick Consideration*, that of the Hundred and Twenty Thousand Children, already computed, Twenty thousand may be reserved for Breed; whereof only one Fourth Part to be Males; which is more than we allow to *Sheep, black Cattle,* or *Swine*; and my Reason is, that these Children are seldom the Fruits of Marriage, *a Circumstance not much regarded by our Savages*; therefore, *one Male* will be sufficient to serve *four Females*. That the remaining Hundred thousand, may, at a Year old, be offered in Sale to the *Persons of Quality* and *Fortune*, through the Kingdom; always advising the Mother to let them suck plentifully in the last Month, so as to render them plump, and fat for a good Table. A Child will make two Dishes at an Entertainment for Friends; and when the Family dines alone, the fore or hind Quarter will make a reasonable Dish; and seasoned with a little Pepper or Salt, will be very good Boiled on the fourth Day, especially in *Winter*.

I have reckoned upon a Medium, that a Child just born will weigh

---

2 Ireland had just suffered three years of poor harvest.

Twelve Pounds; and in a solar Year, if tolerably nursed, encreaseth to twenty eight Pounds.

I grant this Food will be somewhat dear, and therefore very *proper for Landlords*; who, as they have already devoured most of the Parents, seem to have the best Title to the Children.

I have already computed the Charge of nursing a Beggar's Child (in which List I reckon all *Cottagers, Labourers*, and Four fifths of the *Farmers*) to be about two Shillings *per Annum*, Rags included; and I believe, no Gentleman would repine to give Ten Shillings for the *Carcase of a good fat Child*; which, as I have said, will make four Dishes of excellent nutritive Meat, when he hath only some particular Friend, or his own Family, to dine with him. Thus the Squire will learn to be a good Landlord, and grow popular among his Tenants; the Mother will have Eight Shillings net Profit, and be fit for Work until she produceth another Child.

Those who are more thrifty (*as I must confess the Times require*) may flay the Carcase; the Skin of which, artificially dressed, will make admirable *Gloves for Ladies*, and *Summer Boots for fine Gentlemen*.

As to our City of *Dublin*; Shambles³ may be appointed for this Purpose, in the most convenient Parts of it; and Butchers we may be assured will not be wanting; although I rather recommend buying the Children alive, and dressing them hot from the Knife, as we do *roasting Pigs*.

Some Persons of a desponding Spirit are in great Concern about that vast Number of poor People, who are Aged, Diseased or Maimed; and I have been desired to employ my Thoughts what Course may be taken, to ease the Nation of so grievous an Incumbrance. But I am not in the least Pain upon that Matter; because it is very well known, that they are every Day *dying*, and *rotting*, by *Cold* and *Famine*, and *Filth*, and *Vermin*, as fast as can be reasonably expected. And as to the younger Labourers, they are now in almost as hopeful a Condition: They cannot get Work, and consequently pine away for Want of Nourishment, to a Degree, that if at any Time they are accidentally hired to common Labour, they have not Strength to perform it; and thus the Country, and themselves, are in a fair Way of being soon delivered from the Evils to come.

I have too long digressed; and therefore shall return to my Subject. I think the Advantages by the Proposal which I have made, are obvious, and many, as well as of the highest Importance.

For, *First*, as I have already observed, it would greatly lessen the *Number of Papists*, with whom we are yearly overrun.

Secondly, The poorer Tenants will have something valuable of

---

3 A butchers' market.

their own, which, by Law, may be made liable to Distress, and help to pay their Landlord's Rent; their Corn and Cattle being already seized, and *Money a Thing unknown*.

Thirdly, Whereas the Maintenance of an Hundred Thousand Children, from two Years old, and upwards, cannot be computed at less than ten Shillings a Piece *per Annum*, the Nation's Stock will be thereby encreased Fifty Thousand Pounds *per Annum*; besides the Profit of a new Dish, introduced to the Tables of all *Gentlemen of Fortune* in the Kingdom, who have any Refinement in Taste; and the Money will circulate among ourselves, the Goods being entirely of our own Growth and Manufacture.

Fourthly, The constant Breeders, besides the Gain of Eight Shillings *Sterling per Annum*, by the Sale of their Children, will be rid of the Charge of maintaining them after the first Year.

Fifthly, This Food would likewise bring great *Custom to Taverns*, where the Vintners will certainly be so prudent, as to procure the best Receipts for dressing it to Perfection; and consequently, have their Houses frequented by all the *fine Gentlemen*, who justly value themselves upon their Knowledge in good Eating; and a skilful Cook, who understands how to oblige his Guests, will contrive to make it as expensive as they please.

Sixthly, This would be a great Inducement to Marriage, which all wise Nations have either encouraged by Rewards, or enforced by Laws and Penalties. It would encrease the Care and Tenderness of Mothers towards their Children, when they were sure of a Settlement for Life, to the poor Babes, provided in some Sort by the Publick, to their annual Profit instead of Expence. We should soon see an honest Emulation among the married Women, *which of them could bring the fattest Child to the Market*. Men would become as *fond* of their Wives, during the Time of their Pregnancy, as they are now of their *Mares* in Foal, their *Cows* in Calf, or *Sows* when they are ready to farrow; nor offer to beat or kick them, (as it is too *frequent* a Practice) for fear of a Miscarriage.

Many other Advantages might be enumerated. For instance, the Addition of some Thousand Carcasses in our Exportation of barrelled Beef: The Propagation of *Swines Flesh*, and Improvement in the Art of making good *Bacon*; so much wanted among us by the great Destruction of *Pigs*, too frequent at our Tables, and are no way comparable in Taste or Magnificence, to a well-grown fat yearling Child; which, roasted whole, will make a considerable Figure at a *Lord Mayor's Feast*, or any other publick Entertainment. But this, and many others, I omit; being studious of Brevity.

I profess, in the Sincerity of my Heart, that I have not the least personal Interest, in endeavouring to promote this necessary Work; having no other Motive than the *publick Good of my Country, by advancing our Trade, providing for Infants, relieving the Poor, and giving some Pleasure to the Rich.* I have no Children, by which I can propose to get a single Penny; the youngest being nine Years old, and my Wife past Child-bearing.

Jonathan Swift

Activities
- Talk about this with a partner. How does reading this make you feel? Select the three most *compelling*, emotionally striking, sentences. (You might also make a collection of unfamiliar words.)
- Could you use the Swiftian approach and anger to shock a modern audience into seeing your point of view about an injustice (for example, famines in Africa)? Which forms should such a modern protest take, e.g. play, TV report, newspaper article?
- What do you consider to be the limits on people's freedom to express their ideas? Is *anything* acceptable? Who should decide?

LANGUAGE

Introduction

Speakers, readers and writers quickly learn to develop views about the language that they use and that other people use. Language must work by rules in order to succeed at all, but it is hard to know how certain the rules are at particular points. However, everybody has a view about what is correct and what is incorrect and these differences of view can become the basis of arguments about language. Another cause of argument is that different groups use different styles of language, but each group thinks that its ways of talking are more appropriate than anyone else's, so that when members of different groups meet, arguments are liable to develop. The 'meeting' need not be personal; it could be an exchange of views in print.

The point is that language is made up and invented all the time and because it is the means by which we do so much of our living it may become as contested and political a subject as money. Money like language, passes between people as a form of exchange. Some people take the comparison further and think that language (not just individual and fashionable words) can lose value over time. Others think that some languages are less valuable than others. As we write, we are hearing news of how a mother has withdrawn her child from school because some of the languages used there are not considered suitable by her. Consider whether you could lose, educationally, by learning a foreign language, even a bit of one. Is there any sense in the idea that knowledge of any language could disadvantage you?

In this section we have tried to present a variety of ways of arguing about language and, incidentally, one way of arguing about argument! Words become the subject of argument because their meanings cannot be fixed for ever, nor are pronunciations constant either for individuals or for groups. 'The Queen's English' changes and some people see change as the slipping away from a correct high standard to a lower one; others see change as a sign of creativity and health. Some accents can strike us as comical, but not the ones that we use! Language is a comparative thing, so that, in one sense, everyone's view is as good as anyone else's. Language games are played to universal rules but most people seem to prefer to catcall their prejudices from the terrace.

A Journey to the Western Islands

Dr Samuel Johnson, one of the great wits of the eighteenth century, compiled the first dictionary of the English language. He travelled, recording Scotland as if it were a very 'foreign' and unfamiliar part of the United Kingdom. In 1773 Scotland was indeed more foreign to most English people than it is now, but Johnson's stance towards the Scots was not one of innocent curiosity. The Scots had to be inferior, not merely different.

Dr Johnson thinks that Earse is the poorer for never having been written down and thus having regular spelling. Also of course there were no books in Earse in the eighteenth century. What Johnson calls 'Earse' is now called Gaelic.

Of the Earse language, as I understand nothing, I cannot say more than I have been told. It is the rude speech of a barbarous people, who had few thoughts to express, and were content, as they conceived grossly, to be grossly understood. After what has been lately talked of Highland Bards, and Highland genius, many will startle when they are told, that the *Earse* never was a written language; that there is not in the world an Earse manuscript a hundred years old; and that the sounds of the Highlanders were never expressed by letters, till some little books of piety were translated, and a metrical version of the Psalms was made by the Synod of *Argyle*. Whoever therefore now writes in this language, spells according to his own perception of the sound, and his own idea of the power of the letters. The *Welsh* and the *Irish* are cultivated tongues. The Welsh, two hundred years ago, insulted their *English* neighbours for the instability of their Orthography; while the *Earse* merely floated in the breath of the people, and could therefore receive little improvement.

When a language begins to teem with books, it is tending to refinement; as those who undertake to teach others must have undergone some labour in improving themselves, they set a proportionate value on their own thoughts, and wish to enforce them by efficacious expressions; speech becomes embodied and permanent; different modes and phrases are compared, and the best obtains an establishment. By degrees one age improves upon another. Exactness is first obtained, and afterwards elegance. But diction, merely vocal, is always in its childhood. As no man leaves his eloquence behind him, the new generations have all to learn. There may possibly be books without a polished language, but there can be no polished language without books.

That the Bards could not read more than the rest of their countrymen, it is reasonable to suppose; because, if they had read, they could probably have written; and how high their compositions may reasonably be rated, an inquirer may best judge by considering what stores of imagery, what principles of ratiocination, what comprehension of knowledge, and what delicacy of elocution he has known any man attain who cannot read. The state of the Bards was yet more hopeless. He that cannot read, may now converse with those that can; but the Bard was a barbarian among barbarians, who, knowing nothing himself, lived with others that knew no more.

There has lately been in the Islands one of these illiterate poets, who hearing the Bible read at church, is said to have turned the sacred history into verse. I heard part of a dialogue, composed by him, translated by a young lady in *Mull*, and thought it had more meaning than I expected from a man totally uneducated; but he had some opportunities of knowledge; he lived among a learned people. After all that has been done for the instruction of the Highlanders, the antipathy between their language and literature still continues; and no man that has learned only *Earse* is, at this time, able to read.

Samuel Johnson

Activities

● Is it true that writing is the best form of language? Is speaking inferior to writing? If no one could write, what would change in society?

● What are the differences between spoken and written forms of language? Working in small groups, try to note as many differences as you can between speech and writing. Tape yourself telling an anecdote or short story. The next day write the story. Get a partner to transcribe the tape recording and compare that story with the one you wrote.

● Or you might like to write a reply to Dr Johnson as if you were an 'Earse' speaker who had learned to write English. Defend the lack of writing in your language.

● Dr Johnson said, "the man who is tired of London is tired of life". Try substituting your own home place for the word 'London'. Does it ring true? Now see page 43 *The Meaning of Liff.*

Freezing Fog Situation

Clive James - the thinking person's Dame Edna Everage. Essayist, critic, poet, spurious autobiographer and single-handed elevator of TV reviewing. The man who described Patrick Moore's hair as evidence of 'skin-diving in Copydex'. This may, of course, have been sour grapes.

It doesn't matter when the Beeb's weatherman, Mr Fish, wears a jacket that strobes like a painting by Bridget Riley. But it does matter when he warns us about something called a 'freezing fog situation'.

There is no such thing as a freezing fog situation. What Mr Fish means is a freezing fog. In the panic of the moment, when on television, I myself have employed the word 'situation' when it was not strictly necessary. Even now I find myself thinking of Mr Fish as Mr Fish situation. But Mr Fish situation has all day to rehearse his little bit of dialogue situation. There is no excuse for his situation getting into a saying 'situation' situation.

If the BBC, once the guardian of the English language, has now become its most implacable enemy, let us at least be grateful when the massacre is carried out with style. *Ski Sunday* (BBC2) was once again hosted by David Vine. The event was the downhill at Crans-Montana. In their new, filmy ski-suits, the contestants looked like Martian archaeologists who had arrived on earth, discovered a packet of condoms, and had tried them on over their entire body. Müller looked like beating Podborsky's time. Understandably excited, David once again chose words to convey something other than what he meant. "And Müller is inside!" he bellowed. "He is inside Podborsky by a long way!"

There was more of the same on *Superstars* (BBC1). This is the programme in which David Vine has Ron Pickering to assist him in the task of verbal evocation as sportsmen who are well known for being good at one thing strive to be a bit better than mediocre at other things.

The first show of the new series featured 'some of the most famous names and faces in twenty-five years of British sport'. Collectively, these were otherwise referred to as 'the great heroes of sporting legend of all time'. Respectively, they were called things like 'the Gentle Giant' and 'the Blond Bomber'.

Among the few great heroes of sporting legend of all time that I could actually recognise was Bobby Charlton, whose baldy hairstyle is hard to miss. For years now, as one chrome-dome to another, I have been trying to reach Bobby through this column in order to tell him that his cover-up can only work in conditions of complete immobility. If he took up Zen finger-wrestling there might be some chance of retaining his carefully deployed strands in place. But in a 100-yard dash against the Gentle Giant and the Blond Bomber the whole elaborate tonsorial concoction was simply bound to fall apart.

Bobby won the race, arriving at the finishing line with his hairstyle streaming behind his skull like the tail of an under-nourished comet. Seemingly without pausing for breath, Bobby went straight into the mandatory victor's interview with David Vine. It was notable, however, that his coiffure had magically been restored to position - i.e. it was back on top of his head.

Fatuous chat matters less when the sport is worth watching. On *Grandstand* (BBC1) there were amazing scenes from Brighton, where China's number two table tennis player, Kuo-Yao Hua, narrowly defeated China's number four, Liang Ke-Liang. Mercifully the commentators refrained from calling either of these men the Bandy-legged Barbarian or the Moon-faced Marauder. "Ooh my goodness me, you really do run out of things to say!" yelled the stunned voice-over, running out of things to say.

For Kuo and Liang, the table merely marked the centre of the battlefield. They spent most of their time in the audience, returning each other's smashes. "Ooh my goodness me, this chap could almost compete in hurdles as well as table-tennis!" screamed the voice-over brilliantly. This Chap was either Kuo or Liang: when they're so far away it's hard to tell them apart.

In fact the camera gave up the attempt to keep them both in shot. You saw This Chap in the distance returning a smash with a high lob that disappeared out of the top of the frame. There would then be a long pause, finally interrupted by the sound of another smash and the reappearance of the ball in low trajectory on its way back to This Chap. "Who could argue that this is not first-class entertainment?" Nobody, so for God's sake shut up.

Grandstand also featured the Rose Bowl: University of Southern California v. Michigan. It becomes clearer all the time that American football leaves our kind looking tired. A voice-over at our end warned that we might find it "a bit of a mystery to unfathom what's going on". But really it was not all that hard to unfathom. Even when you couldn't follow the American commentators you could tell they were talking sense. The tactics and strategy were engrossing even when you only half-understood them. The spectacle, helped out by action replays of every incident from four different angles, was unbeatable.

Among the many startling aspects of the Rose Bowl was the fact that violence was confined to the field of play. Nor did any of the commentators find it necessary to remark that some of the players were white and others black - perhaps because the same applied to the commentators. This was a nice contrast with *Match of the Day* (BBC1), where an hysterical voice-over was to be heard commending "the two coloured players" for "combining beautifully". The difference between commentating and Colemantating is that a commentator says things you would like to remember and a Colemantator says things you would like to forget.

Clive James
21st January 1979

Activities

● Collect as many inept phrases as you can from one evening's television viewing. Can you find anyone who is particularly spectacular at mangling language?

● Try making a tape which is a send-up of a weather forecaster, a sports commentator or a disc jockey.

● Write a review of a night's viewing, perhaps in the style of Clive James.

The Meaning of Liff

The Meaning of Liff is written by Douglas Adams and John Lloyd. Some readers may well remember Douglas Adams for his *Hitchhiker's Guide to the Galaxy* and other books.

The book we are quoting from is, as you will see from the introduction and extract, a delightful spoof based on possible uses of out-of-the-ordinary words which started out life as place names.

In Life*, there are many hundreds of common experiences, feelings, situations and even objects which we all know and recognize, but for which no words exist.

On the other hand, the world is littered with thousands of spare words which spend their time doing nothing but loafing about on signposts leading to places.

Our job, as we see it, is to get these words down off these signposts and into the mouths of babes and sucklings and so on, where they can start earning their keep in everyday conversation and make a more positive contribution to society.

*And, indeed, in Liff.

Luffenham (n.)
Feeling you get when the pubs aren't going to open for another forty-five minutes and the luffness is beginning to wear a bit thin.

Luffness (n.)
Hearty feeling that comes from walking on the moors with gumboots and cold ears.

Lulworth (n.)
Measure of conversation.
A lulworth defines the amount of the length, loudness and embarrassment of a statement you make when everyone else in the room unaccountably stops talking at the same moment.

Luppitt (n.)
The piece of leather which hangs off the bottom of your shoe before you can be bothered to get it mended.

Lusby (n.)
The fold of flesh pushing over the top of a bra which is too small for the lady inside it.

Luton (n.)
The horseshoe shaped rug that goes round a lavatory seat.

Lybster (n., vb.)
The artificial chuckle in the voice-over at the end of a supposedly funny television commercial.

Lydiard Tregoze (n.)
The opposite of a mavis enderby (q.v.). An unrequited early love of your life who still causes terrible pangs though she inexplicably married a telephone engineer.

Douglas Adams and John Lloyd

Activities

● Using a map of your local area, produce some new entries for *The Meaning of Liff.* As a starter, give definitions for the following West Yorkshire towns: Heckmondwyke, Mytholmroyd, Gomersal, Liversedge.

● Use the words in the extract to produce new meanings which sound equally ridiculous but just might be true.

● Work in groups and use the surnames of people you know to produce a different version. (Be careful not to be too offensive - remember, somebody might be working on your name!)

If ...

Steve Bell is a cartoonist who works for *The Guardian* and specialises in anti-government satire. You could see his work as part of a long tradition of English satire which attacks those with power, stretching from Cruikshank to *Spitting Image.* Cruikshank was an eighteenth century cartoonist whose work satirised those in power by making them look, literally, ridiculous. A similar idea, though not a similar style, can be seen in the work of Gerald Scarfe.

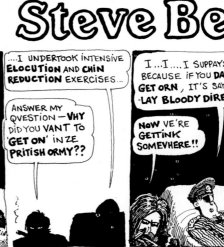

Activities

● Read the cartoon strip dialogue out in pairs. Discuss how important accent is in the way we view one another.

● Research exercise: mine your own background and that of your relatives. How many languages and dialects can you lay claim to?

● Make tape recordings of three different types of accent (consider social class and geography). Discuss what effect these accents have on the audience, e.g. parents, other students. How stereotyped are the responses you get?

Filming in War

Robert Capa took this photo during the Spanish Civil War. It shows the death of a Republican soldier in 1936.

Robert Capa

Activity
- What argument is this photograph making?

Standard English

The Cox Report was written in 1989 by a committee which made recommendations on the teaching of English. The committee followed the work of the Kingman Committee which looked at how English language should be taught. Among other things, language is an extraordinarily potent social weapon: governments are keen to keep track of it.

5.41   Chapter 4 discussed the place of Standard English in the curriculum. Competence in Standard English is clearly a central aim of the English curriculum. What is at issue at this point in our Report is the terminology required for adequate knowledge about Standard English. To understand what Standard English is, terms are required to discuss its forms and functions, and its historical, geographical and social distribution. To illustrate this we provide three brief paragraphs on Standard English: the technical terms which are necessary to write this are in italics.

5.42   'Standard English is usually analysed by linguists as a *dialect* of English. On purely linguistic grounds, it is not inherently superior to other *non-standard dialects* of English, but it clearly has social prestige. This is partly because of the purposes which it now serves: it is the expected language in the education system and other social institutions (such as the courts and business), in almost all published writing, and it has also spread far beyond its historical base in Britain and is used as *an international language* in many parts of the world. Non-standard dialects of English are *regional dialects*: that is, they are relatively restricted in their geographical spread. Standard English used to be restricted in this way: if we look at Standard English as an *historical dialect*, then we find that 200 years ago it had a much smaller number of speakers in England, and had nothing like the geographical spread it has nowadays. Standard English is also a *social dialect*: its use is a marker of social group membership, and the relationship between standard and non-standard dialects and social class in Britain is particularly strong.

5.43   'Although Standard English is not inherently superior to other dialects of English, it is nevertheless true that, because of its long use especially in writing for academic and administrative purposes, the *vocabulary* and to some extent the *sentence syntax* of Standard English have been greatly elaborated. Non-standard dialects have the potential to be so developed, but for social and historical reasons they have not been.

Activities

● Try writing a passage from a history or biology text book in non-standard English. Are there any gains?

● Collect evidence (using taped interviews) of regional forms of English. What about English as spoken in Scotland or Wales?

● With the group, find out what views people hold about the following dialects: Cockney, West Country, Upper Class, Caribbean English. What does this reveal about our attitude to people?

● Organise a group reading of 'Them & [uz]' by Tony Harrison (see page 57). North Country readers of this text may be at an advantage.

Argument

Monty Python's Flying Circus was made for television in the 1970s. The writer-performers defined the comic taste of a generation (now probably your parents and teachers). In the late 1980s the series enjoyed something of a revival.

  Here is a transcript of a television sketch:

Knock Knock

A	Come in. (*B Enters*)
B	Is this the right room for an argument?
A	I've told you once.
B	No you haven't.
A	Yes I have.
B	When?
A	Just now.
B	No you didn't.
A	Yes I did.
B	You didn't.
A	I'm telling you I did.
B	You did not.
A	I'm sorry, is this a five-minute argument or the full half-hour?
B	Oh, just the five-minute one (*sits*).
A	Fine.
B	Thank you.
A	Anyway I did.
B	You most certainly did not.
A	Now let's get one thing quite clear. I most definitely told you.
B	You did not.
A	Oh yes I did.
B	Did not.
A	Did.
B	Didn't.
A	Yes I did.
B	Look, this isn't an argument.
A	Yes it is.
B	No it isn't, it's just contradiction.
A	No it isn't.
B	It is! You just contradicted me.
A	No I didn't.
B	Oh you did.
A	No, no, no, no.
B	You did, just then.
A	No, nonsense.
B	Oh look, this is futile.

A   No it isn't.

B   I came here for a good argument.

A   No you didn't, you came here for an argument.

B   Well an argument's not the same as contradiction.

A   Can be.

B   No it can't; an argument is a connected series of statements to establish a definite proposition.

A   No it isn't.

B   Yes it is - it isn't just contradiction.

A   Look, if I argue with you I must take up a contrary position.

B   But it isn't just saying, "no it isn't".

A   Yes it is.

B   No it isn't. Argument is an intellectual process. Contradiction is just the automatic gainsaying of anything the other person says.

A   No it isn't.

B   Yes it is.

A   Not at all.

B   Now look.

A   (*Thumps bell on desk*) Thank you. Good morning.

B   What?

A   That's it. Good morning.

B   I was just getting interested.

A   Sorry, the five minutes is up.

B   That was never five minutes just now.

A   Yes it was.

B   No it wasn't.

A   Sorry; I'm not allowed to argue any more.

B   What?

A   If you want me go on arguing you'll have to pay for another five minutes.

B   But that was never five minutes just now. Oh, come on, this is ridiculous.

A   I'm very sorry, but I told you, I'm not allowed to argue unless you pay.

B   Oh alright. There you are (*pays*).

A   Thank you. (*Takes money*)

B   Well?

A   Well what?

B   That was never five minutes just now.

A   I've just told you, I'm not allowed to argue unless you've paid.

B   I just paid.

A   No you didn't.

B   I did. I did. I did! I don't want to argue about that.

A Well I'm very sorry but you didn't pay.

B Ah ha! Well, if I didn't pay, why are you arguing. Got you.

A No you haven't.

B If you're arguing I must have paid.

A Not necessarily. I could be arguing in my spare time.

(from a Monty Python transcript)

Activity

- Perform the sketch.

The Telephone Call

Fleur Adcock is a poet. She was born in New Zealand and has an acute sense of the absurd as well as a great tenderness in her description of human relationships (*see* 'The Keepsake').

They asked me "Are you sitting down?
Right? This is Universal Lotteries",
they said. "You've won the top prize,
the Ultra-super Global Special.
What would you do with a million pounds?
Or, actually, with more than a million -
not that it makes a lot of difference
once you're a millionaire." And they laughed.

"Are you OK?" they asked - "Still there?
Come on, now, tell us, how does it feel?"
I said "I just . . . I can't believe it!"
They said "That's what they all say.
What else? Go on, tell us about it."
I said "I feel the top of my head
has floated off, out through the window,
revolving like a flying saucer."

"That's unusual" they said. "Go on."
I said "I'm finding it hard to talk.
My throat's gone dry, my nose is tingling.
I think I'm going to sneeze - or cry."
"That's right" they said, "don't be ashamed
of giving way to your emotions.
It isn't every day you hear
you're going to get a million pounds.

Relax, now, have a little cry;
we'll give you a moment ... " "Hang on!" I said.
"I haven't bought a lottery ticket
for years and years. And what did you say
the company's called?" They laughed again.
"Not to worry about a ticket.
We're Universal. We operate
a Retrospective Chances Module.

Nearly everyone's bought a ticket
in some lottery or another,
once at least. We buy up the files,
feed the names into our computer,
and see who the lucky person is."
"Well, that's incredible" I said.
"It's marvellous. I still can't quite ...
I'll believe it when I see the cheque."

"Oh," they said, "there's no cheque."
"But the money?" "We don't deal in money.
Experiences are what we deal in.
You've had a great experience, right?
Exciting? Something you'll remember?
That's your prize. So congratulations
from all of us at Universal.
Have a nice day!" And the line went dead.

Fleur Adcock

Activities
- In groups of four or five, collect your parents', friends' and
neighbours' junk mail for two weeks. Recompose selected phrases from
the material into a poem which contains infinite promise of riches.
- Find out how to take your name off a junk mailing list. Write
guidelines for your fellow students.

A Second-hand Car Sale

In this passage Steinbeck is not only arguing against the lying
tendencies of car dealers by exposing their sales patter for what it is,
but also points up the innocent dependency of the victims of the
salesmen. Poor people, forced to migrate to California in wrecks of cars
in the 1930s, are heroes of Steinbeck's novel which remains a great
documentary account of that event in American history.

Cars lined up, noses forward, rusty noses, flat tyres. Parked close together.

Like to get in to see that one? Sure, no trouble. I'll pull her out of the line.

Get 'em under obligation. Make 'em take up your time. Don't let 'em forget they're takin' your time. People are nice, mostly. They hate to put you out. Make 'em put you out, an' then sock it to 'em.

Cars lined up, Model Ts, high and snotty, creaking wheel, worn bands. Buicks, Nashes, De Sotos.

Yes, sir. '22 Dodge. Best goddamn car Dodge ever made. Never wear out. Low compression. High compression got lots a sap for a while, but the metal ain't made that'll hold it for long. Plymouths, Rocknes, Stars.

Jesus, where'd that Apperson come from, the Ark? And a Chalmers and a Chandler - ain't made 'em for years. We ain't sellin' cars - rolling junk. Goddamn it, I got to get jalopies. I don't want nothing for more'n twenty-five, thirty bucks. Sell 'em for fifty, seventy-five. That's a good profit. Christ, what cut do you make on a new car? Get jalopies. I can sell 'em fast as I get 'em. Nothing over two hundred fifty. Jim, corral that old bastard on the sidewalk. Don't know his ass from a hole in the ground. Try him on that Apperson. Say, where is that Apperson? Sold? If we don't get some jalopies we got nothing to sell.

Flags, red and white, white and blue - all along the kerb. Used Cars. Good Used Cars.

To-day's bargain - up on the platform. Never sell it. Makes folks come in, though. If we sold that bargain at that price we'd hardly make a dime. Tell 'em it's jus' sold. Take out that yard battery before you make delivery. Put in that dumb cell. Christ, what they want for six bits? Roll up your sleeves - pitch in. This ain't gonna last. If I had enough jalopies I'd retire in six months.

Listen, Jim, I heard that Chevvy's rear end. Sounds like bustin' bottles. Squirt in a couple quarts of sawdust. Put some in the gears too. We got to move that lemon for thirty-five dollars. Bastard cheated me on that one. I offer ten an' he jerks me to fifteen, an' then the son-of-a-bitch took the tools out. God Almighty! I wisht I had five hundred jalopies. This ain't gonna last. He don't like the tyres? Tell 'im they got ten thousand in 'em, knock off a buck an' a half.

Piles of rusty ruins against the fence, rows of wrecks in back, fenders, grease-black wrecks, blocks lying on the ground and a pig-weed growing up through the cylinders. Brake rods, exhausts, piled like snakes. Grease, gasoline.

See if you can't find a spark plug that ain't cracked. Christ, if I had fifty trailers at under a hundred I'd clean up. What the hell is he kickin' about? We sell 'em, but we don't push 'em home for him.

That's good! Don't push 'em home. Get that one in the Monthly, I bet. You don't think he's a prospect? Well kick 'im out. We got too much to do to bother with a guy who can't make up his mind. Take the right front tyre off the Graham. Turn that mended side down. The rest looks swell. Got tread an' everything.

Sure! There's fifty thousan' in that ol' heap yet. Keep plenty oil in. So long. Good luck.

Looking for a car? What did you have in mind? See anything attracts you? I'm dry. How about a little snort a good stuff? Come on, while your wife's lookin' at that La Salle. You don't want no La Salle. Bearings shot. Uses too much oil. Got a Lincoln '24. There's a car. Run forever. Make her into a truck.

Hot sun on rusted metal. Oil on the ground. People are wandering in, bewildered, needing a car.

Wipe your feet. Don't lean on that car, it's dirty. How do you buy a car? What does it cost? Watch the children now. I wonder how much for this one? We'll ask. It don't cost money to ask. We can ask, can't we? Can't pay a nickel over seventy-five, or there won't be enough to get to California.

God, if I could only get a hundred jalopies. I don't care if they run or not.

Tyres used, bruised tyres, stacked in tall cylinders; tubes, red, grey, hanging like sausages.

Tyre patch? Radiator cleaner? Spark intensifier ? Drop this little pill in your petrol tank and get ten extra miles to the gallon. Just paint it on - you got a new surface for fifty cents. Wipers, fan belts, gaskets? Maybe it's the valve. Get a new valve stem. What can you lose for a nickel?

All right, Joe. You soften 'em up an' shoot 'em in here. I'll close 'em, I'll deal 'em or I'll kill 'em. Don't send in no bums. I want deals.

Yes, sir, step in. You got a buy there. Yes, sir! At eighty bucks you got a buy.

I can't go no higher than fifty. The fella outside says fifty.

Fifty. Fifty? He's nuts. Paid seventy-eight fifty for that little number. Joe, you crazy fool, you tryin' to bust us? Have to can that guy? I might take sixty. Now look here, mister, I ain't got all day. I'm a business man but I ain't out to stick nobody. Got anything to trade?

Got a pair of mules I'll trade.

Mules! Hey, Joe, hear this? This guy wants to trade mules. Didn't nobody tell you this is the machine age? They don't use mules for nothing but glue no more.

Fine big mules - five and seven years old. Maybe we better look around.

Look around! You come in when we're busy, an' take up our time an' then walk out! Joe, did you know you was talkin' to pikers?

I ain't a piker. I got to get a car. We're goin' to California. I got to get a car.

Well, I'm a sucker. Joe says I'm a sucker. Says if I don't quit givin' my shirt away I'll starve to death. Tell you what I'll do - I can get five bucks apiece for them mules for dog feed.

I wouldn't want them to go for dog feed.

Well, maybe I can get ten or seven maybe. Tell you what we'll do. We'll take your mules for twenty. Wagon goes with 'em, don't it? An' you put up fifty, an' you can sign a contract to send the rest at ten dollars a month.

But you said eighty.

Didn't you never hear about carrying charges and insurance? That just boosts her a little. You'll get her all paid up in four-five months. Sign your name right here. We'll take care of ever'thing.

Well, I don't know -

Now, look here. I'm givin' you my shirt, an' you took all this time. I might a made three sales while I been talkin' to you. I'm disgusted. Yeah, sign right there. All right, sir. Joe, fill up the tank for this gentleman. We'll give him petrol.

Jesus, Joe, that was a hot one! What'd we give for that jalopy? Thirty bucks - thirty-five wasn't it ? I got that team, an' if I can't get seventy-five for that team, I ain't a business man. An' I got fifty cash an' a contract for forty more. Oh, I know they're not all honest, but it'll surprise you how many kick through with the rest. One guy come through with a hundred two years after I wrote him off. I bet you this guy sends the money. Christ, if I could only get five hundred jalopies! Roll up your sleeves, Joe. Go out an' soften 'em, an' send 'em in to me. You get twenty on that last deal. You ain't doing bad.

John Steinbeck

Activities

● Think of a possession in your family (perhaps a car) that you could advertise. Find examples of classified advertisements. Using some of their most exaggerated features, advertise the article you have chosen. (If you can get hold of a video camera and a group of like minded people, make a TV commercial.)

IDENTITY

Introduction

Ever since the idea was floated that everyone was unique, with the right to have their individuality respected, we have seen and heard a growing volume of argument about how rights are gained and a sense of identity established. People have learned to say who they are and why they matter. That you might be female, or black or young, or that you don't speak in the way that *they* speak all become matters, not for apology for lowly status, but for positive assertion. The idea 'black is beautiful' was a powerful argument because in three words it overturned acceptance of the centuries-old tradition that black was ugly, inferior, or wrong. The term of insult had become a term of pride.

In these extracts you will find a concern with self-knowledge, with knowing who we are and what we can do and why we are significant, even if not unique. Questions of identity may not always rely upon argument, but in the selection that follows argument is essential to the writers, engaged as they are with the world's ideas and assumptions in order to help establish their rights, or the rights of others, to be the people they want to be. In this way we can see that issues of identity can be public issues as much as private ones, for each of us has to form a self that can survive in the world, even if the world hurts or seems absurd. If it does, then luckily we can enjoy, like Billy Liar, the secret consolation of daydreams and ideal images of a society that is free of tension and conflict and into which we can fit with perfect ease, our significance guaranteed. Perhaps, though, the daydreams are not so soft and we are right to argue for less strife and difficulty in being ourselves. Private worlds can affect the public one.

The main themes that we have chosen have to do with identity and culture. For example, Paul Theroux, male, finds himself at odds with the American ideal of manhood, with its emphasis on demonstrative toughness and suspicion of the artistic. Tony Harrison's poem, like Theroux's piece, is full enough of conflict, but conflict between social groups and ways of speaking. Out of these tensions comes clarification of the poet's sense of who he is and where his loyalties lie. Other pieces also seek to resolve a tension in arguing a case or position.

May we leave this introduction with a question? Who has been left out from this section - which groups have been arguing, of late, for their rights to be accepted as they are, and whose arguments have we, apparently, ignored?

Them & [uz]

Tony Harrison is a poet and playwright of some fame (or notoriety) following the broadcast of *V* and *Blasphemers' Banquet* on television. He writes, among other things, about his childhood as a bright working-class boy growing up in Leeds.

Them & [uz]
for Professors Richard Hoggart and Leon Cortez

I
αἰαῖ, ay, ay! . . . stutterer Demosthenes
gob full of pebbles outshouting seas -

4 words only of *mi 'art aches* and ...'Mine's broken,
you barbarian, T.W.!' *He* was nicely spoken.
'Can't have our glorious heritage done to death!'

I played the Drunken Porter in *Macbeth*.

'Poetry's the speech of kings. You're one of those
Shakespeare gives the comic bits to: prose!
All poetry (even Cockney Keats?) you see
's been dubbed by [ʌs] into RP,
Received Pronunciation, please believe [ʌs]
your speech is in the hands of the Receivers.'

'We say [ʌs] not [uz], T.W.!' That shut my trap.
I doffed my flat a's (as in 'flat cap')
my mouth all stuffed with glottals, great
lumps to hawk up and spit out ... *E - nun - ci - ate*!

II
So right, yer buggers, then! We'll occupy
your lousy leasehold Poetry.

I chewed up Littererchewer and spat the bones
into the lap of dozing Daniel Jones
dropped the initials I'd been harried as
and used my *name* and own voice: [uz] [uz] [uz],
ended sentences with by, with, from,
and spoke the language that I spoke at home.
RIP RP, RIP T.W.
I'm *Tony* Harrison no longer you!

You can tell the Receivers where to go
(and not aspirate it) once you know
Wordsworth's *matter/water* are full rhymes,
[uz] can be loving as well as funny.

My first mention in the *Times*
automatically made Tony Anthony!

Tony Harrison

Notes on the poem

i   NB 'αἱαῖ' is Greek and is pronounced 'ay, ay!' A collision of north country English and classical Greek.

ii   Demosthenes was a Greek orator with a stammer which he corrected by speaking with a mouth full of pebbles and shouting louder than the noise of the sea.

iii   Tony Harrison here remembers being asked to read Keats' poetry out loud. He had only read the first four words of the poem when his English teacher mocked the pronunciation and brought his reading to a halt. He (the teacher) was 'nicely spoken', but was it nice to stop the young reader after only four words?

iv   '[ʌs]' This is the phonetic transcription of the word 'us' in 'received' pronunciation, '[uz]' is the Northern version used by the boy Harrison.

v   Daniel Jones was a linguist who classified the different vowel sounds we make in speech, when spelling cannot show the differences. Harrison uses Jones' system by quoting [uz] and [ʌs].

Activities

● Prepare a reading of this poem.

● Collect examples from television or radio advertising of how different accents are used with different products. What is sold in local accents? What is sold using 'RP' the most 'correct' pronunciation?

● This poem can be seen as a counter-argument to the views expressed by Harrison's English teacher. Was the teacher even partly right to act as he did? Could you defend his point of view?

Being a Man

Paul Theroux is a travel writer and novelist who comes from the United States of America. One of his novels, *The Mosquito Coast* was made into a successful film, starring Harrison Ford.

There is a pathetic sentence in the chapter 'Fetishism' in Dr Norman Cameron's book *Personality Development and Psychopathology*. It goes, 'Fetishists are nearly always men; and their commonest fetish is a woman's shoe.' I cannot read that sentence without thinking that it is just one more awful thing about being a man - and perhaps it is an important thing to know about us.

I have always disliked being a man. The whole idea of manhood in America is pitiful, in my opinion. This version of masculinity is a little like having to wear an ill-fitting coat for one's entire life (by contrast, I imagine femininity to be an oppressive sense of nakedness). Even the expression 'Be a man!' strikes me as insulting and abusive. It means: Be stupid, be unfeeling, obedient, soldierly and stop thinking. Man means 'manly' - how can one think about men without considering the terrible ambition of manliness? And yet it is part of every man's life. It is a hideous and crippling lie; it not only insists on difference and connives at superiority, it is also by its very nature destructive - emotionally damaging and socially harmful.

The youth who is subverted, as most are, into believing in the masculine ideal is effectively separated from women and he spends the rest of his life finding women a riddle and a nuisance. Of course, there is a female version of this male affliction. It begins with mothers encouraging little girls to say (to other adults) "Do you like my new dress?" In a sense, little girls are traditionally urged to please adults with a kind of coquettishness, while boys are enjoined to behave like monkeys towards each other. The nine-year-old coquette proceeds to become womanish in a subtle power game in which she learns to be sexually indispensable, socially decorative and always alert to a man's sense of inadequacy.

Femininity - being lady-like - implies needing a man as witness and seducer; but masculinity celebrates the exclusive company of men. That is why it is so grotesque; and that is also why there is no manliness without inadequacy - because it denies men the natural friendship of women.

It is very hard to imagine any concept of manliness that does not belittle women, and it begins very early. At an age when I wanted to meet girls - let's say the treacherous years of thirteen to sixteen - I was told to take up a sport, get more fresh air, join the Boy Scouts, and I was urged not to read so much. It was the 1950s and if you asked too many questions about sex you were sent to camp - boy's camp, of course: the nightmare. Nothing is more unnatural or prison-like than a boy's camp, but if it were not for them we would have no Elks' Lodges, no pool rooms, no boxing matches, no Marines.

And perhaps no sports as we know them. Everyone is aware of how few in number are the athletes who behave like gentlemen. Just as high school basketball teaches you how to be a poor loser, the manly attitude towards sports seems to be little more than a recipe for creating bad marriages, social misfits, moral degenerates, sadists, latent rapists and just plain louts. I regard high school sports as a drug far worse than marijuana, and it is the reason that the average tennis champion, say, is a pathetic oaf.

Any objective study would find the quest for manliness essentially right-wing, puritanical, cowardly, neurotic and fueled largely by a fear of women. It is also certainly philistine. There is no book-hater like a Little League coach. But indeed all the creative arts are obnoxious to the manly ideal, because at their best the arts are pursued by uncompetitive and essentially solitary people. It makes it very hard for a creative youngster, for any boy who expresses the desire to be alone seems to be saying that there is something wrong with him.

It ought to be clear by now that I have something of an objection to the way we turn boys into men. It does not surprise me that when the President of the United States has his customary weekend off he dresses like a cowboy - it is both a measure of his insecurity and his willingness to please. In many ways, American culture does little more for a man than prepare him for modeling clothes in the L. L. Bean catalogue. I take this as a personal insult because for many years I found it impossible to admit to myself that I wanted to be a writer. It was my guilty secret, because being a writer was incompatible with being a man.

There are people who might deny this, but that is because the American writer, typically, has been so at pains to prove his manliness that we have come to see literariness and manliness as mingled qualities. But first there was a fear that writing was not a manly profession - indeed, not a profession at all. (The paradox in American letters is that it has always been easier for a woman to write and for a man to be published.) Growing up, I had thought of sports as wasteful and humiliating, and the idea of manliness was a bore. My wanting to become a writer was not a flight from that oppressive role-playing, but I quickly saw that it was at odds with it. Everything in stereotyped manliness goes against the life of the mind. The Hemingway personality is too tedious to go into here, and in any case his exertions are well-known, but certainly it was not until his aberrant behavior was examined by feminists in the 1960s that any male writer dared question the pugnacity in Hemingway's fiction. All the bullfighting and arm wrestling and elephant shooting diminished Hemingway as a writer, but it is consistent with a prevailing attitude in American writing: one cannot be a male writer without first proving that one is a man.

It is normal in America for a man to be dismissive or even somewhat apologetic about being a writer. Various factors make it easier. There is a heartiness about journalism that makes it acceptable - journalism is the manliest form of American writing and, therefore, the profession the most independent-minded women seek (yes, it is an illusion, but that is my point). Fiction-writing is equated with a kind of dispirited failure and is only manly when it produces wealth - money is masculinity. So is drinking. Being a drunkard is another assertion, if misplaced, of manliness. The American male writer is traditionally proud of his heavy drinking. But we are also a very literal-minded people. A man proves his manhood in America in old-fashioned ways. He kills lions, like Hemingway; or he hunts ducks, like Nathanael West; or he makes pronouncements like, 'A man should carry enough knife to defend himself with,' as James Jones once said to a *Life* interviewer. Or he says he can drink you under the table. But even tiny drunken William Faulkner loved to mount a horse and go fox hunting, and Jack Kerouac roistered up and down Manhattan in a lumberjack shirt (and spent every night of *The Subterraneans* with his mother in Queens). And we are familiar with the lengths to which Norman Mailer is prepared, in his endearing way, to prove that he is just as much a monster as the next man.

When the novelist John Irving was revealed as a wrestler, people took him to be a very serious writer; and even a bubble reputation like Eric (*Love Story*) Segal's was enhanced by the news that he ran the marathon in a respectable time. How surprised we would be if Joyce Carol Oates were revealed as a sumo wrestler or Joan Didion active in pumping iron. 'Lives in New York City with her three children' is the typical woman writer's biographical note, for just as the male writer must prove he has achieved a sort of muscular manhood, the woman writer - or rather her publicists - must prove her motherhood.

There would be no point in saying any of this if it were not generally accepted that to be a man is somehow - even now in feminist-influenced America - a privilege. It is on the contrary an unmerciful and punishing burden. Being a man is bad enough; being manly is appalling (in this sense, women's lib has done much more for men than for women). It is the sinister silliness of men's fashions, and a clubby attitude in the arts. It is the subversion of good students. It is the so-called 'Dress Code' of the Ritz-Carlton Hotel in Boston, and it is the institutionalized cheating in college sports. It is the most primitive insecurity.

And this is also why men often object to feminism but are afraid to explain why: of course women have a justified grievance, but most men believe - and with reason - that their lives are just as bad.

Paul Theroux

Activities

● Take any paragraph of this extract and rewrite it so that is part of an essay called 'Being a Woman'. For example: 'It is very hard to imagine any concept of womanhood that does not belittle men and it begins very early. At the age when I wanted to meet boys ...'

Does your version work as well as the original? Ask a friend for an opinion.

● Do you agree with what Theroux says? Is being a young man as problematic as he asserts it is? How far do you think we are encouraged to behave in stereotypical ways? Does your school or college encourage or challenge such stereotypes? Write a response to Theroux's argument.

● Paul Theroux is writing here of North American culture. Is European culture (including British) any different?

Paul Theroux's Enthusiasms

Here is a reply to Theroux's essay on 'Being a Man'. It is a review of the book which contains the essay, and was written by the British novelist and critic Martin Amis.

'I have always disliked being a man,' writes Paul Theroux, in a brief essay called 'Being a Man'. 'The whole idea of manhood in America is pitiful, in my opinion.' Not only pitiful: also 'stupid', 'unfeeling', 'right-wing', 'puritanical', 'cowardly', 'grotesque', 'primitive', 'hideous', 'crippling' - and 'a bore', too, what's more. Although there is some truth in these iterations, the adult male has no practicable alternative to being a man - certainly no cheap or painless one. But maybe Mr Theroux *has* found a way round being a man (I concluded, towards the end of this hefty selection of occasional pieces, *Sunrise with Seamonsters*). Being a boy!

As a novelist, Theroux is attracted to the dark, the haunted, the hidden; he is also attracted to the theme of childhood, though more for its terrors than its exhilarations. As a literary odd-jobber, however, as a left-handed gun, he is breezy, temperate and mild - often downright sunny. Nothing makes him blue. A tour of a crammed and rotting madhouse in Afghanistan can't spoil his spirits. He contrives to have a fun-filled week on the New York subway, strolling among the mangled Morlocks with the transit police. He even hits it off with John McEnroe.

Sunrise with Seamonsters is full of jaunts and larks and treats and sprees, obsessions, hobbies, self-indulgences. First, there are the trains. Theroux has already written two whole books about trains, but the choo-choos and chuff-chuffs feature prominently in this one too. The Aztec Eagle, The Lake Shore Limited, The London Ferry, The Frontier Mail, The Izmir Express - The Nine Forty-Five! The whistles, the manifests, the long waits and chance buttonholings still provide endless fascination for this dark-spectacled Bradshaw, train-spotting from the wrong side of the glass. Perhaps the most reckless piece in the book is a seduction fantasy (young man, mature woman -

'her sobs of pleasure', etc.), followed by an essay in praise of the older ladies. 'At her age she could know every trick in the book and, if it weren't for her pride ... she could probably make a fortune as a hooker.' *Cor*. The seduction takes place in the South of France. On a train.

Martin Amis

Activities

● Amis achieves his effect through mockery. Can you demolish an argument using the same means? For example, you might take a pro-blood sports article and attack it with a large dose of mockery.
● Re-read the passages by Theroux and Amis. Amis mocks Theroux but does he win the argument? Decide in pairs and write a brief joint paragraph 'Why Amis wins' or 'Why Theroux wins'. Submit your entries to an agreed referee in the class and arrange for her or him to read out the winning name and quote two or three of the supporting paragraphs.
● Write a brief consumers' guide to non-sexist toys suitable for 8 to 11 year olds.

Whoring after English Gods

R. Parthasarathy's piece is interesting because again it is a fusion of language and identity, like a number of other pieces in this book.

It was in my last year at school that I was introduced to Rupert Brooke's poem, 'The Soldier'. Phrases from the poem kept haunting me for the next twelve years, only to stop abruptly one late autumn when I found myself 'under an English heaven'. During those twelve years England had become an obsession. Besides, since leaving school, I had also begun to write poems.

I owe my knowledge and love of the English language to the English and Irish priests at school. To one of them, especially, I am profoundly indebted. Not many years ago, on hearing that he was ill, I wrote a poem. Here it is.

An Englishman, tall, high cheek-bones, rather
anaemic (his trousers showed under his cassock)
romped in the field with the boys. It was he

ten years ago taught me language.
Not so much in class as in the penance study.
Together, we read *The Death of Socrates*.

The last I heard he was convalescing:
he has grown old in England. And the syllables
he taught a boy have grown to poems.

That was the beginning. And the years only helped it to become an obsession. I had entered Don Bosco in my tenth year totally unfamiliar with English. The War was on, and my schooling had been interrupted. I lived with my grandmother for a while in Srirangam, an island in the Kaveri, to which my imagination constantly returned. Often I used to visit an aunt in nearby Tannirppalli, on the road to Kulitalai. The Kaveri gleamed a few kilometres away from her doorstep. The house itself was in a coconut grove, spiked with bamboo and pipal. The cousins were all tomboys, and loved rough, noisy games and play - especially Sundari. We had a stream in the backyard, and Sundari would drop into it like a pebble from an overhanging branch. She must have been twelve then, with long, black eyes and hair dropping to the knees. We used to romp around the backyard, making eerie noises with pipal leaves and bamboos, and cooling our heels in the stream. Looking back I would like to think of it as an Edenic world.

On my return to Bombay, I spent a couple of years in a Hindi school in the northern suburb of Matunga where we lived. The school no longer exists. To this day I do my multiplications in Hindi. For a few years I had a tutor who used to come home three times a week to teach me Tamil. I did not learn much from him, and because he used to pinch my thighs blue, he was asked not to come any more. I regret I did not again have an occasion to learn Tamil till almost twenty years later. At home, Father taught me to recite, in Tamil, the hymns of the Ālvārs, the *Nālāyirappirapantam*, especially the *Tiruvāymoḻi* of Nammāḻvār. Also, with father's help, I was able to get over my fear of English. In the seven years (1944-51) I was at Don Bosco, English had become part of me. Little did I then realise that I had paid an exorbitant price.

In college I read English literature, and wrote unevenly. However, a poem of mine bagged the first prize in a poetry contest for students sponsored by *The Free Press Bulletin*. Later, I showed it to one of my professors, who is himself a poet. He said he liked the poem, and that he had no intention of flattering me. And when I was about to take my leave of him, rather overwhelmed, he said, "I myself don't know whether it's a blessing or a curse to be a poet. Keep writing, all the same." That was another beginning. I was on the first step, and I recalled with pleasure a line of Cavafy's: 'Coming as far as this is not little.'

In August 1962, I received from a friend in England an unusual birthday present: a poem of mine in a special issue of *The Times Literary Supplement*. In an article in the issue, 'Why Write in English? India's Search for Self-expression', the writer remarks, 'Recent literary creation in India, whether in English or the regional languages, has been almost the monopoly of those well-grounded in English, and all literary forms have been profoundly affected by

English models.'

In September 1963, I left for England on a scholarship from the British Council. I was, like most Indians educated in English, certain that I would find myself more or less at home there. I was uneasy in India. And exposed as I was to English ideas and attitudes, I became hypercritical of everything Indian. Indian society was, I felt, deeply neurotic, its feet chained to a grossly exaggerated past. There was, again, something terribly wrong with the Indian character itself. Spiritually bankrupt and powerless to absorb the shocks of the twentieth century, India was a 'nation of sleepwalkers', its people sick in the mind and helpless. The nation had, I kept telling myself, lost its will to live. I decided that England would be my future home. And the English language would help me to belong there. In my ignorance I even hoped for fame as a poet in English. But events were to prove otherwise. The English autumn was a little too much for my hopefully expanding tropical petals. In England, at last, history caught up with me: I found myself crushed under two hundred years of British rule in India. I began to have qualms about my own integrity as an Indian. Had not Emerson said, 'India fell to British character'? My encounter with England only reproduced the by-now familiar pattern of Indian experience in England: disenchantment. Here was an England I was unable to come to terms with. The England I had known and loved existed nowhere, except in my mind. This *other* England I did not know even existed. My disenchantment was total. I felt betrayed. I was no longer a 'body of England's breathing English air'.

I spent my first Christmas in England with an old friend from Bombay, at his flat in Hampstead. We bought a few bottles of Guinness stout and packets of crisps from a pub round the corner. He then put on a record of Ravi Shankar, I think it was *Rāga Bhairavi*. That night was yet another beginning. I had, at last, begun my Indian education. That it should have begun in England was a paradox, but nevertheless, an obvious commonplace. A part of me finally died in England. Should I have made the journey at all? It had broken my life in two. Who was I to blame, fate or the historical situation? It was my tragedy, and the tragedy of men like me, to have grown up in the twilight of the Raj. I was thirteen when the Union Jack folded up over India. Since then, the English have gone home; but the English language is still with us. Nothing is more incongruous than the presence of the English language in India. English will always remain a foreign language to us. I realised that I could never function as a poet in England. I felt embittered, and was inclined to agree with Victor Anant that we are all 'Macaulay's bastards'. I had a taste of this unsuspected foreignness of English soon after I arrived in England. At St Pancras station, after a pint of beer, I asked the barmaid, "A matchbox, please." To my surprise, she smiled and asked, "You mean a box of matches, luv?" And when I asked her what the difference was, she smiled again, and explained. So much for my use of the English language, for which I was undeservedly praised by my English friends. One of them had said, "Your own use of English is like that of an educated Englishman. If you think it isn't, try to draw up a list of the ways in which it differs, or examples of where you have failed to communicate. That is a challenge. I don't think you can fail to conclude that any differences that exist are not significant." He was right. I did get my matchbox, after all.

R. Parthasarathy

Activity

● Interview in depth someone around your age (a classmate?). Try to write an account of some of the things that have shaped their personality and outlook.

Hints

1 To get beyond the favourite colour/zodiac sign exchange, persuade your subject to bring in photographs, old toys, and so on and to talk not only of the past but also of hopes for the future. This will not be a short exercise. You may need several hours of interviews before your subject begins to open up.

2 Be careful. Respect privacy. Remember that most people have some areas of their lives that they don't feel able to talk about.

Neither Hindu nor Muslim

Bulleh Shah (1680-1756), a Punjabi poet, makes a plea for something
we all have felt: the desire to be recognised as ourself and not be
labelled or placed in a pigeon-hole.

ہندو نہیں، نہ مُسلمان

Neither Hindu nor Muslim
I sit with all on a whim.
Having no caste, sect, or creed,
I am different indeed.
Neither thirsty nor quite slaked,
I am not dressed nor naked.
I do not laugh, do not cry,
and neither stay nor go by.
I am not sinner or saint
knowing nor sin nor restraint.
Bulleh tries hard to shirk
the embrace of Hindu and Turk.

Bulleh Shah

Activities
- Try to get this poem translated into *at least* one other language. Be
prepared to talk about how you got the job done.
- What is the original language? Can you find anyone to read it for you?
- Notice the poem's rhyme pattern. Can you follow it? (See how line

one rhymes with line two, line three with line four and so on.) Does this add force to the poem's argument?
● Try to write a twelve-line poem. Can you match the form of this poem - your poem will also be about yourself and each line will be 'neither ..... nor ....' in form.

In a Bar

Ian Oxley wrote this piece while a school student, as part of a GCSE course. We include it because it strikes us as a work of extraordinary force and sensitivity.

The waitress bent down to wipe the table. She had a cloth in her right hand which she circled around the table in quick, light movements. Then she reached over towards some empty glasses by the side of the table.

The glasses were a mixture: of tall straight glasses with many melting ice cubes and curious objects like mini-umbrellas and multi-coloured straws and flags inside them, wine glasses instantly recognisable by their round shapes standing on thin tubes of glass leading towards their bases, and most abundant of all forty beer glasses, no ice, no straws, no umbrellas.

The waitress looked at them in a curiously affectionate manner. She gave a sigh as she reached out and picked them up, clutching them between fingers and thumbs so that each one pushed on another one's sides.

A lot can be learned from a pile of empty glasses if you are willing to look close enough: Who was drinking from them. How many there was in the group. Their taste. Their budget.

With the glasses in tight grasp she made her way back to the bar. In doing so she had to brush past groups of young men, standing with glasses in their hands; they were all drinking, smoking, laughing, joking. Without attracting any wolf-whistles or any groping hands she skilfully crossed the room. Quite noticeably this was not easy, it looked like a highly practised skill; as if this barmaid valued herself too highly to flirt with customers just to persuade them to come again.

As a barmaid she seemed out of place. She was obviously a local. Her brown eyes and straight dark hair gave her naturally creamy sunned skin a subtlety that so acutely was lacking in tanned foreigners whose two week colour change so harshly contrasts with their features and hair. She wore no make up. No tarty clothes and was very quiet. The pub however wore make up: modern decorating, green walls, artificial plants, framed prints on the walls, a glass case with a display of jumpers and ties for sale, a 'video juke-box' that created more noise and chaos than even that of the clients.

At the bar she pressed a small glass on an upturned bottle. The glass filled and she turned, to accept, over the counter, some light coins and an old note in exchange. She reached over and the man at the other side of the bar smiled. She smiled back. Her smile was cold and radiated none of the emotions that the man had hoped for. He scuttled away and disappeared into the crowds instead of sitting at the bar as he planned.

She opened a till and placed in it the note; the coins went into her pocket.

Behind her was an open doorway in which a man stood blocking out the view behind him. He flew into a rage. His eyes were bulging out of his dark weathered skin. He darted to where she was and began to shake his finger at her as he spoke to her in Greek. She ran off towards the doorway crying and wiping her eyes on her blouse arm.

Through the open doorway a door slammed. The man, who it was now apparent was the owner took over the girl's job and began to serve drinks. He did this with authority that set him worlds apart from the girl's uninvolved cold manner. He chatted to his customers as he took their money. He was warm, friendly, but somehow he seemed artificial - switching from reprimanding the girl to make small talk over the bar was done with an unhidden degree of professionalism.

Now the girl had gone and the man was serving drinks I could see right into the hallway beyond the bar. It was a telling scene: a bare light bulb hung from a white ceiling full of cracks, dust and squashed mosquitoes. There was a telephone - large, old fashioned and black - leading from one corner of the room to another by a pile of washing. The floors were concrete and there was a large door, obviously not in use at the end of the doorway near a staircase with more dirty washing piled against it like a pile of glasses in a bar - you can tell a lot from a pile of washing if you look carefully.

Everything fell together in that moment. These were real people conducting real lives in their homes. But outside, in the bar, these people were in a false environment created by themselves out of need. The bar was a different world from the one in the hallway. The man who had done well and seemed to be the owner had the ability to cope with this, he had adapted well. The girl was a different kind of person. She had not adapted well to the false world of the bar. It is not necessary to say she is not good at putting on an act and that the man is. It would be more accurate to say that she is unwilling to put on an act. She tries to live her life whilst at work. The man had sacrificed this in order to live a better life outside it. In coping with his work he lives better, whereas the girl can not see this.

How awful I thought, that these people must fit with the clients rather than the clients making an effort to fit in with the natural environment of the foreign bar staff. Surely the people standing around drinking would benefit from the experience of getting to know real locals, being real in a real part of a foreign country. But this would require effort. The effort to be patient, to submit to foreign cultures and perhaps even to make an attempt to understand their language rather than have everyone speaking to them in English. This was clearly impossible, I thought, as I looked around the pub. It was these people who were forcing the locals to be false. I was one of them; this worried me. This had been the year when I had hoped to make an effort. My German was at the point where, perhaps, I could be understood without demanding that I should be spoken to in English, my French was such that I reasonably could have tried to be inconspicuous. But Greece? I've heard of 'pi' in maths, 'alpha', 'gamma', 'delta', and 'rho' in physics but this was hardly much of a start.

I stood up to go. I thought to myself that you can learn a lot from languages. Like empty glasses and the dirty washing. Take German, isn't it just so obvious what kind of a nation they are simply by listening to their language? As I understand it the stereotype typical German is supposed to be calculated, well planned, strong and forceful. Now I wouldn't claim for one minute that this is a fair representation; I don't know many Germans but I'm sure, many of them are as compassionate as the Italian race are said to be. But can't you see my point, when I say that the language of a country fits the stereotype of the people? Perhaps the stereotypes do not emerge from meeting people but from their language. Or perhaps the shape of the language shapes the people? After all we all think in our own language so perhaps this can affect personality. Could the subordinating conjunctions, separable prefixes, strong verbs, strict word order and punctuation rules sending verbs all over the place in the German language lead to better manufacturing of quality precision cars? Could the round endings on Italian words and their flowing style of speech lead to compassionate understanding of human love? Could the Americans' 'think big' strategy have led from the way they pronounce their vowels? It seems a reasonable conclusion to draw. It is much fairer to group nationalities together than colours. After all people of the same nationality share, not only language but also culture, way of life and in many cases religion. Whereas no matter what the colour of your skin, in this day and age, you could have been raised anywhere, without any connection to one country. Even if stereotypes are fair (which they probably are not) there is no valid case for making an evaluation due to colour.

Ian Oxley

Activities

- What are the main propositions here? How far does careful description add to the force of the writer's observations?
- Select a place you know well. Go and observe it; allow your reflections and arguments to grow from a careful description of some aspects of what you see.
- List three other types of location, in addition to bars, where humanity might profitably be observed in some variety. Do it.

The Seal who Became Famous

James Thurber was one of the great humorous writers of the United States, and his illustrations are as famous as his writing. He often used the form of the fable, which can be potent in the cause of argument, especially when given an off-beat treatment, such as we find here. The fable achieves its point by presenting stories about people as if they were animals.

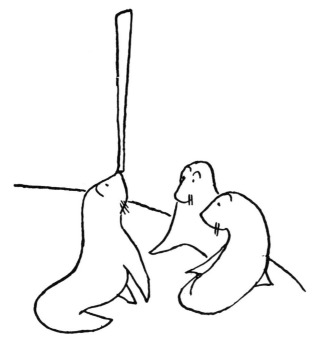

A seal who lay basking on a large, smooth rock said to himself: all I ever do is swim. None of the other seals can swim any better than I can, he reflected, but, on the other hand, they can all swim just as well. The more he pondered the monotony and uniformity of his life, the more depressed he became. That night he swam away and joined a circus.

Within two years the seal had become a great balancer. He could balance lamps, billiard cues, medicine balls, hassocks, taborets, dollar cigars, and anything else you gave him. When he read in a book a reference to the Great Seal of the United States, he thought it meant him. In the winter of his third year as a performer he went back to the large, smooth rock to visit his friends and family. He gave them the Big Town stuff right away: the latest slang, liquor in a golden flask, zippers, a gardenia in his lapel. He balanced for them everything there was on the rock to balance, which wasn't much. When he had run through his repertory, he asked the other seals if they could do what he had done and they all said no. "O.K.," he said. "Let's see you do something I can't do." Since the only thing they could do was swim, they all plunged off the rock into the sea. The circus seal plunged right after them, but he was so hampered by his smart city clothes, including a pair of seventeen-dollar shoes, that he began to founder at once. Since he hadn't been in swimming for three years, he had forgot what to do with his flippers and tail, and he went down for the third time before the other seals could reach him. They gave him a simple but dignified funeral.

Moral: Whom God equipped with flippers should not monkey around with zippers.

James Thurber

Activities
● Devise a different moral from the one that Thurber has provided here.
● Re-write this fable, keeping to the original as much as possible, but providing a different ending and a different moral. Does it work as effectively as the original?

SEEING OTHERS

Introduction

As humans we are all fairly nosey. We like looking over the fence, as it were, at our neighbours. The only trouble is we often manage to make ourselves look good by making other, different, people look bad. Stereotyping 'others' of course is very easy - many governments have managed to persuade their subjects that they are not too badly ruled by endlessly pointing out the evils of another country. The 'evils' of others have often served as the justification for massive spending on armaments, as in Ronald Reagan's dubbing of the USSR as the 'evil empire'. The Communist side has often reasoned in a similar way, spurred on by describing 'capitalism' as necessarily evil.

Looking at other people is of course deeply fascinating, although it is quite definitely rude to stare! For all that, our writers here *have* stared. They've often looked beyond a surface impression and tried to interpret the 'otherness' that they see. To look on other people, other cultures, it is not necessary to travel far, though some of our writers have travelled across the world, V.S. Naipaul from Trinidad to West Africa, Clive James from Australia to England. It might be that there is just as good travel writing waiting to be written within a short distance of each of us. All that we need is careful observation, a willingness to learn and above all an ability to suspend judgement, to be prepared to respect the unfamiliar.

The assumptions we make in describing other people can often, if we are honest, tell us a great deal about ourselves. In the end a prejudiced attack on someone else is an attack on ourselves.

Islam and the West

Edward Said is a Palestinian by birth, and a professor of English Literature in the United States. We think that this piece of writing is apt in the 1990s, as the West struggles to find ways of relating to Islam.

In order to make a point about alternative energy sources for Americans, Consolidated Edison of New York (Con Ed) ran a striking television advertisement in the summer of 1980. Film clips of various immediately recognizable OPEC personalities - Yamani, Qaddafi, lesser-known robed Arab figures - alternated with stills as well as clips of other people associated with oil and Islam: Khomeini, Arafat, Hafez al-Assad. None of these figures was mentioned by name, but we were told ominously that 'these men' control America's sources of oil. The solemn voice-over in the background made no reference to who 'these men' actually are or where they come from, leaving it to be felt that this all-male cast of villains has placed Americans in the grip of an unrestrained sadism. It was enough for 'these men' to appear as they have appeared in newspapers and on television for American viewers to feel a combination of anger, resentment, and fear. And it is this combination of feelings that Con Ed instantly aroused and exploited for domestic commercial reasons, just as a year earlier Stuart Eizenstat, President Carter's domestic policy adviser, had urged the president that "with strong steps we [should] mobilize the nation around a real crisis and with a clear enemy - OPEC."

There are two things about the Con Ed commercial that, taken together, form the subject of this book. One, of course, is Islam, or rather the image of Islam in the West generally and in the United States in particular. The other is the use of that image in the West and especially in the United States. As we shall see, these are connected in ways that ultimately reveal as much about the West and the United States as they do, in a far less concrete and interesting way, about Islam. But let us first consider the history of relationships between Islam and the Christian West before we go on to examine the current phase.

From at least the end of the eighteenth century until our own day, modern Occidental reactions to Islam have been dominated by a radically simplified type of thinking that may still be called Orientalist. The general basis of Orientalist thought is an imaginative and yet drastically polarized geography dividing the world into two unequal parts, the larger, 'different' one called the Orient, the other, also known as 'our' world, called the Occident or the West. Such divisions always come about when one society or culture thinks about another one, different from it; but it is interesting that even when the Orient has uniformly been considered an inferior part of the world, it has always been endowed both with greater size and with a greater potential for power (usually destructive) than the West. Insofar as Islam has always been seen as belonging to the Orient, its particular fate within the general structure of Orientalism has been to be looked at first of all as if it were one monolithic thing, and then with a very special hostility and fear. There are, of course, many religious, psychological, and political reasons for this, but all of these reasons derive from a sense that so far as the West is concerned, Islam represents not only a formidable competitor but also a latecoming challenge to Christianity.

Edward Said

Activities
- List what seem to you the main images of Islam and Islamic life and practice.
- As a group invite an Islamic person to speak to you. Decide in advance the kinds of questions you would like answering and include a

summary of them in your letter.
● Make two display boards of: Islam, Christianity, Communism or a political party in your own country. On one board try to show a positive image, on the other a negative. (The tabloid press might prove useful here. Note the adjectives that are used, for example, to describe left-wing politicians in British tabloid newspapers.)

Falling Towards England

You have met Clive James elsewhere in this book (page 40). He is an Australian writer and broadcaster whose flamboyant style has won him many admirers and some enemies.

... In England it was very cold, colder than I had ever known. The customs men did a great deal of heavy-handed chaffing about how you cobbers couldn't really call this a winter, ho ho, and what we would look like if there really was a winter, har har, and so on. Their accents were far funnier than their sense of humour. They all seemed to have stepped out of the feature list of an Ealing comedy for the specific purpose of unpacking our luggage and charging us extra for everything in it. My own luggage consisted mainly of one very large suitcase made of mock leather - i.e. real cardboard. This compendium was forced into rotundity by a valuable collection of tennis shorts, running shorts, Hawaiian shirts, T-shirts, Hong Kong thong rubber sandals, short socks, sandshoes and other apparel equally appropriate for an English winter. The customs officer sifted through the heap twice, the second time looking at me instead of at it, as if my face would betray the secret of the illicit fortunes to be made by smuggling unsuitable clothing across half the world.

As the people all around me were presented with huge bills, I gave silent thanks for being in possession of nothing assessable for duty. The ship's fool - a pimply, bespectacled British emigrant called Tanner who was now emigrating back the other way - was near tears. In Aden and Port Said he had bought, among other things, two tape recorders, a Japanese camera called something like a Naka-mac with a silver box full of lenses, a portable television set slightly larger than an ordinary domestic model but otherwise no different except that it had a handle, a stuffable leather television pouffe for watching it from, a hi-fi outfit with separate components, and a pair of binoculars so powerful that it frightened you to look through them, especially if you saw Tanner. Most of this gear he had about his person, although some of it was packed in large cardboard boxes, because all this was happening in the days before miniaturisation, when an amplifier still had valves. The customs officer calculated the duty owing and confronted him with the total, at which he sat down on his boxed telescope and briefly wept. It was more money than he had in the world, so he just signed away the whole mountain of gear and walked on through a long door in the far side of the shed.

A few minutes afterwards I walked through the same door and emerged in England, where it was gently snowing on to a bus full of Australians. There was a small cloud in front of my face which I quickly deduced to be my breath. The bus was provided by the Overseas Visitors' Club, known for short as the OVC. The journey by ship, the bus ride to London and a week of bed and breakfast in Earls Court were all part of the deal, which a few years later would have been called a Package, but at that time was still known as a Scheme. The general thrust of the Scheme was to absorb some of the culture shock, thus rendering it merely benumbing instead of fatal. As the bus, which strangely insisted on calling itself a coach, headed north - or west or east or wherever it was going, except, presumably, south - I looked out into the English landscape and felt glad that I had not been obliged to find my way through it unassisted.

The cars seemed very small, with no overhang at either end. A green bus had 'Green Line' written on it and could therefore safely be assumed to be a Green Line bus, or coach. The shops at the side of the road looked as if they were finely detailed painted accessories for an unusually elaborate Hornby Dublo model railway table top layout. Above all, as well as around all and beyond all, was the snow, almost exactly resembling the snow that fell in English films on top of people like Alastair Sim and Margaret Rutherford. What I was seeing was a familiar landscape made strange by being actual instead of transmitted through cultural intermediaries. It was a deeply unsettling sensation, which everybody else in the coach must have shared, because for the first time in twelve thousand miles there was a prolonged silence. Then one of the wits explained that the whole roadside façade would fold down after we had roared by, to reveal factories manufacturing rust-prone chromium trim for the Standard Vanguard. There was some nervous laughter and the odd confident assurance that we were already in the outskirts of London. Since the outskirts of London were well known to embrace pretty well everywhere in the south of England up to the outskirts of Birmingham, this seemed a safe bet.

A few ploughed fields presented themselves so that the girls, still pining for members of the ship's crew, might heave a chorus of long sighs at the bunny rabbits zipping across the pinwhale corduroy snow. After that it was one continuous built-up area turning to streetlight in the gathering darkness of what my watch told me was only mid-afternoon. Enveloped in many layers of clothing, people thronging the footpaths seemed to be black, brown or, if white and male, to have longer hair than the females. High to the left of an arching flyover shone the word WIMPEY, a giant, lost, abstract adjective carved from radioactive ruby.

There was no way of telling, when we arrived, that the place we were getting off at was called Earls Court. In those days it was still nicknamed Kangaroo Valley but there were no obvious signs of Australia except the foyer of the OVC, crowded with young men whose jug ears stuck out unmistakably from their short haircuts on either side of a freckled area of skin which could be distinguished as a face, rather than a neck, only by the presence of a nose and a mouth. Here I was relieved to find out that I had been assigned to the same dormitory room as my cabin mates, at a hostel around the corner. So really we were still on board ship, the journey from the OVC foyer around the corner to the hostel being the equivalent of a brisk turn around the deck, while carrying a large suitcase.

The snow was falling thickly enough to replenish a half-inch layer on the footpath, so that my black Julius Marlowe shoes could sink in slightly and, I was interested to notice, be fairly rapidly made wet. It hadn't occurred to me that snow would have this effect. I had always assumed snow to be some form of solid. In the hostel I counted up my financial resources. They came to just a bit more than ten pounds in English money. Ten pounds bought quite a lot at that time, when eight pounds a week was a labourer's living wage and you could get a bar of chocolate for threepence, a chunky hexagonal coin which I at first took to be some form of washer and then spent a lot of time standing on its edge on the bedside table while figuring out what to do next. Improvising brilliantly, I took some of the small amount of money over and above the ten pounds and invested in an aerogramme, which I converted into a begging letter and addressed to my mother, back there in Sydney with no telephone. Her resources being far from limitless, I did my best not to make the letter too heartrending, but after it was finished, folded and sealed I had to leave it on the radiator for the tears to dry out, after which it was wrinkled and dimpled like an azure poppadum.

Dinner in the hostel made me miss the ship-board menu, which until then I would have sworn nothing ever could. What on earth did a spotted dick look like before the custard drowned it? A glass mug of brown water was provided which we were assured was beer. I sipped fitfully at mine while everybody else watched. When I showed no signs of dengue fever or botulism, they tried theirs. Having rolled inaccurately into my bunk, I discovered, like my two cabin mates, that I couldn't sleep for the silence of the engines.

Clive James

Activities
- Which is your favourite paragraph in the passage? Give two or three reasons for choosing it.
- Sit down with a partner and share your remembered first impressions of a place you have visited. (This need not be either very far away nor indeed a terribly earnest task!)
- Write your own personal list of the six most enjoyable phrases in the piece as a whole. A list of ours would definitely include: 'Wimpey ... carved from radioactive ruby' and 'a face rather than a neck ...'
- Go out and collect some first impressions from people who have recently moved into your area. (NB. This may be people who have moved towns, counties or even countries, but the more you can find and interview the better.)

Paris and the Parisians

The writer seems to us to be almost apologetic about her choice of subject. It seems as though, as a woman, she does not wish to be associated with fashion as trivia. (You may wish to question our choice of pieces here as male editors of this book.)

  We think that the piece shows something of the importance of dress in terms of establishing identity and asserting ourselves in the world. Though Fanny Trollope seems to disapprove of an obsession with fashion, do you think she exhibits it in writing about it?

Considering that it is a woman who writes to you, I think you will confess that you have no reason to complain of having been overwhelmed with the fashions of Paris: perhaps, on the contrary, you may feel rather disposed to grumble because all I have hitherto said on the fertile subject of dress has been almost wholly devoted to the historic and fanciful costume of the republicans. Personal appearance, and all that concerns it, is, however, a very important feature in the daily history of this showy city; and although in this respect it has been made the model of the whole world, it nevertheless contrives to retain for itself a general look, air, and effect; which it is quite in vain for any other people to attempt imitating. Go where you will, you see French fashions; but you must go to Paris to see how French people wear them.

  The dome of the Invalides, the towers of Notre Dame, the column of the Place Vendôme, the windmills of Montmartre, do not come home to the mind as more essentially belonging to Paris, and Paris only, than does the aspect which caps, bonnets, frills, shawls, aprons, belts, buckles, gloves, - and above, though below, all things else - which shoes and stockings assume, when worn by Parisian women in the city of Paris.

It is in vain that all the women of the earth come crowding to this mart of elegance, each one with money in her sack sufficient to cover her from head to foot with all that is richest and best; - it is in vain that she calls to her aid all the *tailleuses, coiffeuses, modistes, couturières, cordonniers, lingères,* and *friseurs* in the town: all she gets for her pains is, when she has bought, and done, and put on all and everything they have prescribed, that, in the next shop she enters, she hears one *grisette·* behind the counter mutter to another, 'Voyez ce que désire cette dame anglaise;' - and that, poor dear lady! before she has spoken a single word to betray herself.

Fanny Trollope
1836

Activities

● Conduct a survey to find out how important dress is as an issue. Focus on something like: school uniform; modern extremes of fashion; the amount of money people are prepared to spend on clothes; the dress expectations and conventions of particular careers. In groups of three or four, agree a particular angle, research it and present your findings to the whole group in as interesting a way as you can.

● In groups, write a list of ten reasons why the media assume women are more interested than men in fashion. Then discuss them as a whole class.

Europe's Myths of the Orient

Adrienne Rich is an American poet. Rana Kabbani, an Islamic writer, lives in England. Neither the poem nor the prose paragraph makes any concessions to simple language but the pieces repay careful reading and re-reading.

I can never romanticize language again
never deny its power for disguise
for mystification
but the same could be said for music
or any form created
painted ceilings beaten gold
worm-worn Pietàs reorganizing victimization
frescoes translating violence
into patterns so powerful and pure
we continually fail to ask are they true for us.

Adrienne Rich

The idea of travel as a means of gathering and recording information is commonly found in societies that exercise a high degree of political power. The traveller begins his journey with the strength of a nation or an empire sustaining him (albeit from a distance) militarily, economically, intellectually and, as is often the case, spiritually. He feels compelled to note down his observations in the awareness of a particular audience: his fellow-countrymen in general, his professional colleagues, his patron or his monarch. Awareness of this audience affects his perception, and influences him to select certain kinds of information, or to stress aspects of a country that find resonances in the culture of his own nation. His social position also colours his vision, and (since he often belongs to a leisured class, which enables him to embark on voyages which are both expensive and prestigious) he usually represents the interests and systems of thought in which he was schooled. ...

Rana Kabbani

Activities
- In pairs either:
1 Focus on the poem, or
2 Focus on the paragraph.
Decide what you think are the three most difficult phrases. In small groups, try to work out their meaning. Then discuss it in class.
- Kabbani is a woman writer. Why do you think she uses 'he'? Can you find other examples of this?
- Without writing a 'what I did on my holidays' piece, try to write an account of how it felt to be in a particular place away from home. You may wish to describe, argue, observe, reflect and narrate about people, their habits, food and customs.
- In what ways did you compare things with home? What did you feel about things such as: landscape, buildings, flora and fauna? Keep the focus of your piece on your own feelings and judgements.

The Crocodiles of Yamoussoukro

V. S. Naipaul is a Trinidadian writer of world stature. His novels include: *A Bend in the River*, *A House for Mr Biswas* and *The Enigma of Arrival*.

I travel to discover other states of mind. And if for this intellectual adventure I go to places where people live restricted lives, it is because my curiosity is still dictated in part by my colonial Trinidad background. I go to places which, however alien, connect in some way with what I already know. When my curiosity has been satisfied, when there are no more surprises, the intellectual adventure is over and I become anxious to leave.

It is a writer's curiosity rather than an ethnographer's or journalist's. So while, when I travel, I can move only according to what I find, I also live, as it were, in a novel of my own making, moving from not knowing to knowing, with person interweaving with person and incident opening out into incident. The intellectual adventure is also a human one: I can move only according to my sympathy. I don't force anything; there is no spokesman I have to see, no one I absolutely must interview. The kind of understanding I am looking for comes best through people I get to like. And in the Ivory Coast I moved in the main among expatriates, white and black. I saw the country through them and through their varied experience.

One of these expatriates was Terry Shroeder, the public affairs officer of the American embassy. He was in his late forties, and a bachelor, a slender, handsome man with the kind of melancholy that attracts and resists women. He was going to retire early from the foreign service. The Ivory Coast was his last posting but one, and he was at the very end of his time there. It was Terry who had given me the phrase about 'a little bit of coffee and a little bit of cocoa'. He admired the economic achievements of the Ivory Coast. But he also had a feeling for its African side.

It was Terry who at our first meeting told me that there was in the Ivory Coast a famous and very old African sage who was the president's spiritual counsellor. The sage was open to other consultation as well, and Terry would have liked me to see him. But the sage was unfortunately 'hospitalized,' and remained so during my time in the Ivory Coast. The name of the sage was Amadou Hampaté Bâ. He had been in his time an ambassador, and a member of an important Unesco[1] body; but his fame in the Ivory Coast was spiritual, and rested on his mastery of arithmology and other esoteric studies. Terry knew him well enough to visit him in hospital, and he always referred to him as Mr Hampaté Bâ ('Hampaté' not far in sound from 'Humpty'). Hampaté Bâ was a Muslim from Mali, to the north; but he had a large place in his heart for African religion. 'Islam is my father, but Africa is my mother' - this, according to Terry, was one of Hampaté Bâ's well-known sayings. Another saying was: 'Whenever an old man dies in Africa, a library has burned down.'

At our first meeting Terry also told me about someone who was doing research among the village witch-doctors or medicine men. Some of these men did possess knowledge of a sort. They could deal in an African way with African neuroses; they also knew about herbs and poisons. They were secretive about the poisons. Their

[1]Unesco: United Nations Educational, Scientific and Cultural Organisation

knowledge of poisons made them feared and was one of the sources of their power.

This talk of poison made me think of the Caribbean islands on the other side of the ocean. In the old days, on the slave plantations there, constantly replenished with 'new Negroes' (as they were called) from places like the Ivory Coast, poison had been one of the special terrors of slaves and slave-owners. Some poisoner was always about; in the slave underground or underworld, the hidden Africa of the plantations, someone could usually be found with a stock of poison; and a vengeful slave could do terrible things. In Trinidad in 1794 a hundred Negroes were poisoned on the Coblenz estate in Port of Spain, and the estate had to be abandoned. In 1801, when the estate was bought by the emigré Baron de Montalembert, a poisoner went to work again, and in the first month of his proprietorship the baron lost 120 of the 140 'seasoned' Negroes he had put in.

As much as poison, the plantation owners in the Caribbean feared African magic. Slavery depended on obedience, on the acceptance by the slave of the logic of his position. A persuasive magician, awakening African instincts, could give his fellows a sense of the unreality of the workaday world, and could incite normally docile and even loyal slaves to rebellion. Magicians, once they were identified, were treated with great severity. In Trinidad and Martinique they could be burned alive.

Magic and poison - in the old documents of the islands, they had seemed like the weapons of despair; and they probably had been. Here in the Ivory Coast they were part of a world that was still whole. The African culture that was officially promoted, and could at times seem to be only a source of tourist motifs, was an expression of African religion. Even in the masks in the souvenir shops, even in the dances beside the swimming pool of the Forum Golf Hotel, there was a feeling of awe, a radiation of accepted magical practices. Men here knew another reality; they lived easily in a world of spirit and spirits.

And it was Terry Shroeder who introduced me to Arlette. Arlette was a black woman from Martinique. Her French, beautifully enunciated, revived all my schoolboy love of the language. She was in her late thirties or early forties, a big woman, full of other friendship, generous with her time and knowledge; she was to make me understand many things about the country. She had married an Ivorian, whom she had met in Paris, and she had lived for twenty years in the Ivory Coast. She was divorced now; her former husband had gone to Gabon, the newest French African land of oil and money. Arlette worked in an arts department of the university in Abidjan. She lived by herself; she had many friends in the foreign community; I felt she feared solitude. She was an expatriate - expatriates in the Ivory Coast were black as well as white.

V.S. Naipaul

Activities
- Discuss:

1 ˙ the notion that 'magic' and 'poison' are African arts which run quite counter to European ideas of 'civilisation' and decency';

2 that 'magic' and 'poison' are understandable as legitimate means with which to combat the evil of slavery;

3 that 'magic' and 'poison' are misleading terms as much meaning can be lost translating from one culture to another. In this case, English speakers had also violently 'translated' many Africans into another, alien culture. It might be that the adult world relentlessly translates the youthful world in just such ways.

- 'Whenever an old man dies in Africa, a library has burned down.'

1 What do you think is meant by this?

2 Do you think we in the West alternately neglect and sentimentalise our old people? Find evidence.

3 When your 'library' has burned down, what do you want it to have contained wisdom about?

Subterranean Gothic

Paul Theroux is a writer you have already met (page 58). You might like to read some of his travel writing and also watch the video of his story, *The Mosquito Coast*. You will probably sense some of his irritability with contemporary North American life in some of its less attractive aspects.

It is the obvious vandalism on the subways that conveys the feeling of lawlessness. Indeed, the first perception of subway crime came with the appearence of widespread graffiti in 1970. It was then that passengers took fright and ridership, which had been declining slowly since the 'fifties, dropped rapidly. Passengers felt threatened, and newspapers gave prominence to subway crime. Although the 'CC' line is over thirty-two miles long a passenger will be alarmed to hear that a crime has been committed on it, because this is *his* line, and the proprietorial feeling of a rider for his line is as strong as a jungle dweller's for his regular path. Subway passengers are also very close physically to one another, but this is a city in which people are accustomed to quite a lot of space. On the subway you can hear the breathing of the person next to you - that is, when the train is at the station. The rest of the time it is impossible to hear anything except the thundering of the train, which is equally frightening.

"Violence underground attracts more coverage in the papers, but it is foolish to imagine the subway is some sort of death trap." This statement was not made by anyone in the New York Transit Authority, but by Nadine Joly, the twenty-eight-year-old head of the Special Paris Metro Security Squad. She was speaking about the Paris Metro, but her sentiments are quite similar to those of Edward Silberfarb of the Transit Authority Police.

"The interest in subway crime is much greater than in street crime," Mr Silberfarb said. "Crime actually went down six per cent in September, but the paper reversed the statistic and reported it as having gone up. Maybe they're looking for headlines."

Paul Theroux

Activities
● Make a photographic record of graffiti. Can you discover any main themes (e.g. sex, politics, sport)? Does the theme, if any, depend on location?
● If you wished to embarrass a visiting Martian by supplying false information, what misleading tips would you give her/him/it about how to behave on the underground? (E.g.- it is customary to shake as many people by the hand as you can and wish them good day.) Write a list of such 'rules'.
● Talk to old people about their attitude to crime - then carry out a survey to find people who have personal experience of burglary, or other crimes. What conclusions can you draw? (For example, are people's common fears well grounded in fact?) NB: This should be undertaken with sensitivity, tact and respect towards the older people you interview.

The Journey and the Book

Jonathan Raban is amongst other things a very successful travel writer who once took a small boat down the Mississippi River. His round Britain book, *Coasting*, coincided with Paul Theroux's *The Kingdom By the Sea*. The two books make interesting comparative reading.

The English travel books of the '20s and '30s were, Mr Fussell says, written in the Indian summer of what is now a dead form. Evelyn Waugh, Graham Greene, Norman Douglas, D. H. Lawrence, Robert Byron were the last masters of an art which was to be killed off by politics and the tourist industry. History had put them in a unique position. Never had England seemed so frowsty and constricting as in the period immediately after the Great War. The very word 'abroad' had come to assume a dreamlike, talismanic quality. It had been conceived in the frozen trenches of Flanders and brought to birth in the tired and spiritless streets of Britain's postwar industrial cities. It was raised, umbrella-fashion, over a whole cluster of concepts - of sunlight, liberty, innocence, sexual passion, the fantastic and the healing. When the English writer bought his ticket to sail on the cruise ship or ride on the famous Blue Train, which went from Victoria Station all the way to the Riviera, his real destination was a more restorative idea than a place on the map.

Most important of all, his nationality equipped him with a point of view which made 'abroad' singularly containable as a literary construct. Four hundred years of imperial experience had given the travelling Englishman a very clear idea of where he stood in the world - bang at its moral centre. Foreigners, by definition, were funny, untrustworthy and childlike. To be English and abroad was to be the one tight-minded, right-minded sensibility at large in a confused society where more or less everything was comically lax and wrong. That may have been a deplorable attitude in the realm of international politics, but it was a useful misapprehension to be under when it came to writing books. Snobbishly alert to the small nuances of social behaviour, quick to spot the 'anomalous' details which form the basic grist of travel writing, the Englishman was, in more senses than one, a privileged observer.

It was only when they were abroad, though, that Mr Fussell's literary travellers were ever likely to be mistaken for typical Englishmen. There was something anomalous about each of them in their insecure tenancy of the upper-middling reaches of the class system. They were climbers, like Waugh, or sliders, like Norman Douglas. At home, they stuck out as 'queer', 'not quite', or 'on the make', or simply Papist. In foreign parts, their Englishness was restored to them intact, a comfortable, fictional identity woven in superior Harris tweed.

Jonathan Raban

Activities
● Is travel writing dead? Look at some Sunday newspapers. Go to a bookshop and/or library and ask. Report back. Find out who the most popular writers are.
● Assume the identity of a 'foreigner'. Write about your own area as if the people living there (including yourself) are: 'funny, untrustworthy and childlike'.

PERSUASION

Introduction

We give this section a title with less assurance than some of the other sections. This is so because all arguments are acts of persuasion in some sense - as arguers we want our voices to be heard, believed and even acted upon. We have already included some examples of persuasion, but this section catches something of the enormous *variety* of persuasion that comes our way, whether it be the delight of an unusual idea, as in Primo Levi's piece on weightlessness, or a proposition of how the world comes to be. We also discovered lots of persuasion coming up in novels and poems (there's a novel actually called *Persuasion* but that's another story). Sometimes the language of persuasion is simple, straightforward and direct as if we needed to be convinced by not having to think too hard. In these examples assertion comes into play as the main agent of persuasion, but in other examples there is a greater reliance on the use of evidence and careful thought. Subtlety may be as persuasive as assertion, but it cannot be denied that eloquent and powerful language can do much to change our minds and influence our actions. See how Andrew Marvell seeks to persuade his mistress to yield to his urgent desires in the poem 'To his Coy Mistress'. The end and purpose of his argument may be familiar enough, but look at the care and craft with which he presents it!

We hope that your sharing with us the arguments in this book has given you greater confidence in the ability to defend your own position and to use your own voice to fight for what matters to you. It is often asserted that it is natural to tell stories in order to instruct and delight and to argue. We assert that it is just as natural to argue, maybe even more so. At all events, arguing is a very basic and time-honoured form of discourse and we would like to end this final introductory essay with some ancient Greek writing which uses questions and answers in order, apparently, to discover the truth. In this extract Plato (the writer) makes Socrates (who was his teacher) argue powerfully in favour of expert opinion, but we do not necessarily agree with Socrates, though only in argument could we hope to persuade him that he is wrong. The point is that the issue remains open, from Plato's time to ours.

Expert Opinion

Socrates: Well then, what do you make of my standard illustration? A man is training to be an athlete, and taking his training seriously. Now, does he pay attention to the praise and criticism of anybody and everybody, or does he confine his attention to one man only, I mean the man who happens to be his medical adviser or professional trainer?

Crito: Just to the one man.

Socrates: In that case, he ought to take to heart the praises and criticisms of that one man alone, and disregard popular opinion.

Crito: Obviously.

Socrates: And all his activities, his training and his diet, should be determined by the decision of this one man who is his supervisor and an expert, and not by the general opinion of the public at large.

Crito: That's right.

Socrates: Good. Now our athlete will surely come to harm, won't he, if he disobeys this man, disregards his favourable and unfavourable comments, and instead regards as valid the opinions of the majority, who are not experts?

Crito: Of course he will come to harm.

Socrates: And what is the nature of this harm? What part of our disobedient athlete does it affect?

Crito: His body, of course: it's his body he'll be ruining.

Socrates: Quite right. Lets go through all the other standard illustrations, Crito: the answer in each case will be similar, and the reasoning will also apply to the questions at issue now, which are questions of morality and immorality, of honour and dishonour, of good and evil. The problem is whether we should follow popular opinion in these matters and allow ourselves to be intimidated by it, or whether we should respect the opinion of a single person, the expert - if one exists - in preference to that of everyone else put together. If we do not follow the one man, then we shall maim and mutilate that part of us which is made better by moral behaviour and worse by immoral behaviour. Or am I talking nonsense?

Crito: No, Socrates, I don't think so.

Socrates: Well now, take the part of us which is made better by healthy activities and worse by unhealthy activities: suppose we ruin ourselves by taking the advice of laymen, is life still worth living after we have ruined that part of us? The part we are referring to is the body, isn't it?

Crito: Yes.

Socrates: Well then, is life still worth living when the body is ruined and useless?

Crito: Definitely not.

Socrates: Then what about the part of us which is improved by moral behaviour and damaged by immoral behaviour? Is life worth living when that part is ruined? Or are we to assume that whatever this part of us is, which has to do with morality, it is of less importance than the body?

Crito: Certainly not.

Socrates: It's more important, then?

Crito: Much more.

Socrates: In that case, my friend, we should take no notice whatever of popular opinions on the subject of morality; we should listen only to the expert. That expert should be the one in authority, the one standard of truth. So, going back to your proposal that we should take account of public opinion in the matters of justice, honour and goodness, my immediate reaction is that it is an ill-founded proposal.

Plato

Weightless

Primo Levi, of Turin in Italy, was a survivor of Auschwitz, the Nazi death camp in Poland. This piece, whilst not obviously an argument, does seek to persuade us of the strangeness of the fact that we adapt to weightlessness with ease.

What I would like to experience most of all would be to find myself freed, even if only for a moment, from the weight of my body. I wouldn't want to overdo it - just to hang suspended for a reasonable period - and yet I feel intensely envious of those weightless astronauts whom we are permitted to see all too rarely on our TV screens. They seem as much at ease as fish in water: they move elegantly around their cockpit - these days quite spacious - propelling themselves forward by pushing gently off invisible walls, and sailing smoothly through the air to berth securely at their work place. At other times we have seen them conversing, as if it were the most natural thing - one of them 'the right way up' the other 'upside down' (but of course in orbit there is neither up nor down). Or we have seen them take turns to play childish games: one flicks a toffee with his thumbnail, and it flies slowly and in a perfectly straight line into the open mouth of his colleague. We have seen an astronaut squirt water from a plastic container into the air: the water does not fall or disperse but settles in a roundish mass which then, subject only to the weak forces of surface tension, lazily assumes the form of a sphere. What do they do with it then? It can't be easy to dispose of without damaging the delicate structures upholding its surface.

I wonder what it would take to make a documentary that would link together these visions, transmitted by some miracle from the satellites that flash past above our heads and above our atmosphere. A film like that, drawn from American and Soviet sources, and with an intelligent commentary, would teach everybody so much. It would certainly be more successful than the nonsense that is put out today, more successful too than porno movies.

I have also often wondered about the experiments, or more

particularly the simulation courses which aspiring astronauts have to undergo and which journalists write about as if they were nothing out of the ordinary. What sense is there in them? And how is weightlessness simulated? The only technique imaginable would be to close the candidates in a vehicle in free-fall: a plane or an elevator such as Einstein postulated for the experiment designed to illustrate the concept of special relativity. But a plane, even in a vertical fall, is braked by the resistance of the air, and a lift (or rather, a fall) has additional frictional forces acting on the cable. In both cases, weightlessness (or *abaria* to the die-hard classicists) would not be complete. And even in the best case - the quite terrifying scenario of a plane dropping like a stone from a height of five or ten or twenty miles, perhaps with an additional thrust from the engines in the final stages - the whole thing would last no more than a few tens of seconds: not enough time for any training or for measuring physiological data. And then there would be the question of stopping ...

And yet almost all of us have experienced a 'simulation' of this decidedly non-terrestrial sensation. We have felt it in a childhood dream. In the most typical version, the dreamer becomes aware with joyous amazement that flying is as easy as walking or swimming. How could you have been so stupid as not to have thought of it before? You just scull with the palms of your hands and - hey presto - you take off from the floor, moving effortlessly; you turn around, avoiding the obstacles; you pass skilfully through doors and windows, and escape into the open air: not with the frenetic whirring of a sparrow's wings, not with the voracious, stridulant haste of a swallow, but with the silent majesty of the eagles and the clouds. Where does this presentiment of what is now a concrete reality come from? Perhaps it is a memory common to the species, inherited from our proto-bird-like aquatic reptiles. Or maybe this dream is a prelude to a future, as yet unclear, in which the umbilical cord which calls us back to mother earth will be superfluous and transparent: the advent of a new mode of locomotion, more noble even than our own complicated, unsteady, two-legged style with its internal inefficiencies and its need of external friction between the feet and the ground.

From this persistent dream of weightlessness, my mind returns to a well-known rendition, of the Geryon episode in the seventeenth canto of the *Inferno*. The 'wild beast', reconstructed by Dante from classical sources and also from word-of-mouth accounts of the medieval bestiaries, is imaginary and at the same time splendidly real. It eludes the burden of weight. Waiting for its two strange passengers, only one of whom is subject to the laws of gravity, the wild beast rests on the bank with its forelegs, but its deadly tail floats 'in the void' like the stern-end of a Zeppelin moored to its pylon . At first, Dante was frightened by the creature, but then that magical descent to Malebolge captured the attention of the poet-scientist, paradoxically absorbed in the naturalistic study of his fictional beast whose monstrous and symbolic form he describes with precision. The brief description of the journey on the back of the beast is singularly accurate, down to the details as confirmed by the pilots of modern hang-gliders: the silent, gliding flight, where the passenger's perception of speed is not informed by the rhythm or the noise of the wings but only by the sensation of the air which is 'on their face and from below'. Perhaps Dante, too, was reproducing here unconsciously the universal dream of weightless flight, to which psychoanalysts attribute problematical and immodest significance.

The ease with which man adapts to weightlessness is a fascinating mystery. Considering that for many people travel by sea or even by car can cause bouts of nausea, one can't help feeling perplexed. During month-long spells in space the astronauts complained only of passing discomforts, and doctors who examined them afterwards discovered a light decalcification of the bones and a transitory atrophy of the heart muscles: the same effects, in other words, produced by a period of confinement to bed. Yet nothing in our long history of evolution could have prepared us for a condition as unnatural as non-gravity.

Thus we have vast and unforeseen margins of safety: the visionary idea of humanity migrating from star to star on vessels with huge sails driven by stellar light might have limits, but not that of weightlessness: our poor body, so vulnerable to swords, to guns and to viruses, is space proof.

Primo Levi
(Translated from the Italian by Piers Spencer)

Primo Levi died on 11 April 1987, after a fall at his home in Turin.
His death was reported by Italian newspapers as apparent suicide.

Activities

● Find enough words and phrases in this piece to produce a collage poem. Work in pairs. We suggest that your subject focus is weightlessness but you may see alternatives.

● Find an account of the phenomenon of weightlessness in a science text book. Compare versions. Which do you prefer? NB: Primo Levi was himself a scientist - a distinguished chemist.

● Make out a plea to the Creator of humankind that is an argument for why we should be re-designed so that we can become weightless at will.

The Face of War

Martha Gellhorn has been a war correspondent of great distinction, covering conflicts from the Spanish Civil War through to Vietnam, and beyond. She is also a novelist. This piece was written in 1986 and is the introduction to a collection of her reportage.

The first report in this book was written forty-nine years ago. After a lifetime of war-watching, I see war as an endemic human disease, and governments are the carriers. Only governments prepare, declare and prosecute wars. There is no record of hordes of citizens, on their own, mobbing the seat of government to clamour for war. They must be infected with hate and fear before they catch war fever. They have to be taught that they are endangered by an enemy, and that the vital interests of their state are threatened. The vital interests of the state, which are always about power, have nothing to do with the vital interests of the citizens, which are private and simple and are always about a better life for themselves and their children. You do not kill for such interests, you work for them.

I am suspicious of governments - with a few admirable exceptions - and their version of vital interests. If they were doing their jobs properly, governments would concentrate on seeing that their countries functioned well, to the best advantage of the largest number of citizens: they would not lavish huge chunks of the communal wealth on armaments and economize on the needs of the people. Whether rich or poor or middling, all governments have money for war and every year, more and more, all governments have enormous sums of money to stockpile the weapons of war. And all of them, democratic or despotic, existing on their people's earnings, grudge money for services to the people. We live in an over-armed, underfed world.

To get a war started, you need an aggressor, a government so ambitious, so greedy that the vital interests of its state require foreign conquest. But an aggressor government sells its people the project of war as a defensive measure: they are being threatened, encircled, pushed around: enemies are poised to attack them. It is sadly easy to make people believe any lies; people are pitifully gullible, subject to instant flag-waving and misguided patriotism. And once a war has started, the government is in total control: the people must obey the orders of their government, even if their early induced enthusiasm has waned. They also see that however needlessly the war started, it would be better not to lose it.

The nation or nations that are attacked have no choice except to fight the aggressor. But would not competent governments have seen the menace and taken early action to prevent the aggressor from

completing preparations for war? It is probable that Hitler could have been stopped in 1936, when he reoccupied the Rhineland in violation of the Locarno Pact. Surely the Falklands war could have been avoided by intelligent foresight? Governments are more competent at waging war than preventing it. And, when you get right down to it, war is not so terrible for governments, the people at the top, the people in charge. Their power increases, and governments thrive on power; they have the excitement, the enhanced importance and none of the hardships. They are not ordered to fight or work in factories; miraculously they are not wounded or killed like ordinary people; they are too valuable to live on pinched rations. Until the Second World War, when its unique monstrousness changed the rules, governments paid no more grievous penalty for losing a war than losing their jobs. The Kaiser simply retired to a small rural palace.

Martha Gellhorn

Activities

● Would you wish to see the abolition of the army, navy and airforce? Do you think that Martha Gellhorn would wish countries to disarm entirely? What evidence is there in the text?

● Draw up a list of what you see as the essential functions of any government, e.g. it can compel people: to go to school when young; to pay taxes; to obey its laws.

What are the responsibilities of government? This question is probably probably best tackled in a group, especially to start with.

Genesis: verses 24 - 28

This extract has been included because it represents a very powerful view of the relationship between animals and humankind and between the natural world and ourselves. It provides a religious justification for humans having power - 'dominion' over the natural world.

24 ¶ And God said, Let the earth bring forth the living creature after his kind, cattle, and creeping thing, and beast of the earth after his kind: and it was so.

25 And God made the beast of the earth after his kind, and cattle after their kind, and every thing that creepeth upon the earth after his kind: and God saw that *it was* good.

26 ¶ And God said, Let us make man in our image, after our likeness: and let them have dominion over the fish of the sea, and over the fowl of the air, and over the cattle, and over all the earth, and over every creeping thing that creepeth upon the earth.

27 So God created man in his *own* image, in the image of God

created he him; male and female created he them.

28 And God blessed them, and God said unto them, Be fruitful, and multiply, and replenish the earth, and subdue it: and have dominion over the fish of the sea, and over the fowl of the air, and over every living thing that moveth upon the earth.

29 ¶ And God said, Behold, I have given you every herb bearing seed, which *is* upon the face of all the earth, and every tree, in the which *is* the fruit of a tree yielding seed; to you it shall be for meat.

30 And to every beast of the earth; and to every fowl of the air, and to every thing that creepeth upon the earth, wherein *there is* life, *I have given* every green herb for meat: and it was so.

31 And God saw every thing that he had made, and, behold, *it was* very good. And the evening and the morning were the sixth day.

Activities

● The first question here has to do with the language and origin of this piece. This is the King James translation of the Old Testament of the Bible and was written some three hundred and fifty years ago. Find a more modern version and see how the two versions differ. Which words have changed? Have the ideas changed along with the words? Which do you prefer?

● According to this version of events, man is given dominion over the earth. Re-read Chief Seattle's Reply (page 16) and discuss these two apparently opposing points of view.

● What evidence is there to suggest that this text would not satisfy a rather stern modern examiner in terms of punctuation and grammar? Re-write an extract using modern conventions of layout and punctuation.

● What about vegetarianism? Is there anything in this passage on which to base an argument for or against?

Zen and the Art of Motor Cycle Maintenance

The novel, or journal, follows the author and his son on one motorcycle and two friends, John and Sylvia, on another, as they ride across the United States together. John and Sylvia are 'artistic' and do not care to know, from the point of their being artistic, how their motorcycle works. Here, in this passage, Pirsig begins to try to understand how such intelligent people can become alienated from the technology that supports us all.

... Other things fit in too. They talk once in a while in as few pained words as possible about 'it' or 'it all' as in the sentence, 'There is just no escape from it.' And if I asked, 'From what?' the answer might be 'The whole thing,' or 'The whole organized bit,' or even 'The system.'

Sylvia once said defensively, 'Well, *you* know how to *cope* with it,' which puffed me up so much at the time I was embarrassed to ask what 'it' was and so remained somewhat puzzled. I thought it was something more mysterious than technology. But now I see that the 'it' was mainly, if not entirely, technology. But, that doesn't sound right either. The 'it' is a kind of force that gives rise to technology, something undefined, but inhuman, mechanical, lifeless, a blind monster, a death force. Something hideous they are running from but know they can never escape. I'm putting it way too heavily here but in a less emphatic and less defined way this is what it is. Somewhere there are people who understand it and run it but those are technologists, and they speak an inhuman language when describing what they do. It's all parts and relationships of unheard-of things that never make any sense no matter how often you hear about them. And their things, their monster keeps eating up land and polluting their air and lakes, and there is no way to strike back at it, and hardly any way to escape it.

That attitude is not hard to come to. You go through a heavy industrial area of a large city and there it all is, the technology. In front of it are high barbed-wire fences, locked gates, signs saying No Trespassing, and beyond, through sooty air, you see ugly strange shapes of metal and brick whose purpose is unknown, and whose masters you will never see. What it's for you don't know, and why it's there, there's no one to tell, and so all you can feel is alienated, estranged, as though you didn't belong there. Who owns and understands this doesn't want you around. All this technology has somehow made you a stranger in your own land. Its very shape and appearance and mysteriousness say, 'Get out.' You know there's an explanation for all this somewhere and what it's doing undoubtedly serves mankind in some indirect way but that isn't what you see. What you see is the No Trespassing, Keep Out signs and not anything serving people but little people, like ants, serving these strange, incomprehensible shapes. And you think, even if I were a part of this, even if I were not a stranger, I would be just another ant serving the shapes. So the final feeling is hostile, and I think that's ultimately what's involved with this otherwise unexplainable attitude of John and Sylvia. Anything to do with valves and shafts and wrenches is a part of *that* dehumanized world, and they would rather not think about it. They don't want to get into it. ...

Robert M. Pirsig

Activities
● In groups try to identify a structure near you (e.g. factory, farm, power station) that does not appear to allow or welcome visitors. Use a combination of letters, interviews and other research methods, in an attempt to demystify your chosen structure to the wider group.

- Find some examples of writing about a technology which interests you and share them with the group. Give them the texts and let them ask you, as the expert, real questions.
- Consider some attitudes in one or more of your friends which you find hard to understand or sympathise with. Try to write your way to some glimmering of understanding, however tentative.

Battering and Boiling -
This is the Age of the Wind

Much of the power of this piece, we think, derives from the sensational picture. In this book you will find other pictures which, we feel, argue a point of view.

We sleep these days as seamen must have done in the cabins of an old tea-clipper. Our weather-ears are cocked, and soon the noises begin: something like distant cannon-fire comes booming down the chimney; the slates become restless, and shift; windows rattle, interior doors slam shut and then slam open again; tin cans bounce down the street, trees creak. Our partners turn and mumble in their sleep. What is it? Only the wind.

The earth is wrapped in 560 million million tons of air. Wind is simply air in motion. It can be very pleasant - stimulating, life-enhancing, life-giving, the subject of odes. The civilisation of the Indian sub-continent would not exist without the monsoon wind which delivers the summer rain. In Rome in August the sea breeze, the *ponente*, enlivens Romans like a glass of cool white wine. But now, in northern Europe, it has become hard to see this beneficence in wind. Some of this 560 million million tons of air has become extremely volatile. It lashes out at us like a tyrant with a personal grievance. In two days last week it killed 46 Europeans, 18 of them British, a toll equivalent to a railway disaster. In January's gale, 46 people in Britain died. The damage from both, in Britain alone, is expected to cost £5bn to put right.

Other parts of the world may scoff at our dismay. Wind along the coasts of the Americas or in the Bay of Bengal has always had murderous tendencies. A cyclone in Calcutta in 1737 destroyed 20,000 boats and drowned 200,000 people. Another, in much the same area in 1970, killed 300,000 people in Bangladesh. But Europe has always seen wind as a decorative and useful substance. Zephyrs, balmy breezes, little cherubs with puffed-out cheeks - blowing hard in the corners of maps to disperse sailing fleets to

'Making us feel uneasy, perhaps a little anxious ... even prey to dread':
the promende at Weston-super-Mare, Monday 26 February

colonial treasure and conquest. Before steam displaced it, wind was
the great engine of commerce. England got its first windmill in the
12th century. By the mid-18th century, at what might be called the
height of the Wind Age, there were probably 100,000 of them
scattered across Europe.

Perhaps we are entering a Wind Age of a more hostile kind. We
remember our surprise that morning three autumns ago, when trees
which had grown secure in the earth for centuries lay horizontally
across fields, parks and streets, suddenly feeble things. Now it has

happened again and again. Scaffolding flies apart, houses lose their roofs, streets become rivers and the sea boils up and over the headland.

Why is it happening? According to meteorologists, the recent gales began off the eastern seaboard of the United States where an extremely cold airstream from the Arctic collided with moist, warmer air from the south. This collision is not in itself unusual. Wind is the result of a conflict in air temperatures. Around the Equator, warm air expands and rises and flows in the only direction possible, towards the Poles. Meanwhile, cool air flows from the Poles to replace it. If the Earth were as smooth and still as an apple, all would be monotonously simple: winds high above our heads would flow constantly towards the Poles, while winds on the Earth's surface would flow from them. But mountain ranges get in the way. The Earth, spinning on its axis, sends moving bodies in the Northern hemisphere to the right and in the Southern to the left. We are girdled by a great river of wind.

Fine: but why have our winds become so severe? Nobody can say, but, as with all apparently new and disturbing phenomena, we are told that both the phenomenon and our concern are old. According to Professor Hubert Lamb, of the University of East Anglia's climatic research unit, periods of great storms affect Britain and northern Europe in 100 year cycles, in the years around the turn of centuries. By the study of shipping and civic records and private diaries, Professor Lamb has concluded that savage weather swept Britain in the 1590s, 1690s, 1790 and 1890s.

The effect of sun-spots? A new Ice Age? Global warming? Nobody can be sure, but it seems likely that Britain will have to fortify itself for more of the same in the new decade, and perhaps not only in terms of coastal defence works and more solid houses: the wind may alter our psychology. In his book on the history of the wind, *Heaven's Breath*, Lyall Watson writes: 'A fresh breeze can be exhilarating, clearing the air, blowing sometimes, it seems, clean through us, carrying away obstructions that lie in the way of perfect freedom of mind. But anything more than a strong breeze becomes annoying... We have a surprisingly low threshold to wind - almost as though at a certain speed the skin begins to transmit warning signals to the brain, making us feel uneasy, perhaps a little anxious and irritable, even prey to dread.'

Ian Jack
4 March 1990

Activities
● Underline one statement from the text which you think most nearly captures the force of argument of the picture.

- Collect, as a group, images which support your view of something about which you feel strongly.

or

- Make your own image (e.g. in the form of collage) or photographic essay - for instance you might wish to show that graffiti can be fun.
- Other pictures in this book form part of various arguments. Choose two pictures and in each case:

a) state what you think the argument is;

b) give your own personal reactions in the form of a poem or a short talk.

Children and Cartoons - their cult following

For many years now parents, teachers and individual members of the community have been interested and concerned about what children and young people read. Books have been written, surveys compiled and 'recommended' booklists printed. Research within this area has been vital for those actively involved in choosing positive anti-racist and anti-sexist resources. However, this interest in what children read and how it influences them, has not been balanced with an interest for what children watch on television.

Children's TV has changed and developed over the last 10 years and in some ways the quality of the programmes has improved. Gone are the days of 'Andy Pandy', 'CrackerJack' and 'Thunderbirds'. Instead new brand of TV exists for more children and for more hours of the day.

The introduction of American-based cartoons such as He-Man, She-Ra, Thundercats and Ulysses 21 now dominate our TV screens, similarly the toys and item-related products crowd our shops. Children insist that their lunch boxes feature Skeletor, or their duvet cover has to have She-Ra. The product-related material is endless as is the children's demand for it. These new brands of cartoon depict a violent storyline, which, for the most part is filled with throw-away lines spoken by larger-than-life characters. All in all the cartoons are badly animated, incredibly complex to comprehend (apart from the tedious fighting scenes) and very boring to watch. However, it is far too easy to simply dismiss these cartoons as 'bad' television, because the many messages contained within such programmes are both subtle and insiduous.

Within all of the cartoons the racist imagery and overtones are unmistakable. The heroes and heroines and the defenders of the 'good' are white. They boast blonde hair, blue eyes and sun-tanned faces. The female characters are usually scantily clad, with wasp like waists, which perpetuate an image of beauty that is most definitely white and European. She-Ra's long blonde flowing hair and blue eyes are of course complemented by 'He-Man's' tanned, over-developed muscles, his mass of tidy, but wavy hair and yet again his strong, blue, piercing eyes. The 'baddies' however, are nearly always shrouded in darkness, dressed in black or grey costumes and inhabit dark and gloomy caves usually below the ground's surface. Often the characters are not depicted as 'Black' but they are never depicted as white.

On a recent 'Right to Reply' programme (August 1987) where the topic of such cartoons was discussed at length, the creator of 'He-Man' stated that 'as there were no black heroes then there should be no black baddies'. Some may say that's an acceptable statement, but why are there no black heroes and secondly why are the 'baddies' never depicted as white? In one episode of 'He-Man and the Masters of the Universe' a character called 'Mumrah' (a revived Eyyptian mummy) was depicted as black and ugly. The character has a large, broad nose, full lips and large wide eyes. There was no doubt that in the eyes of the creators ugliness and evilness are related to non-European features. In other words the image of ugliness that they had created was based on African/Afro-Caribbean features.

Apart from the character depictions present within such series, the story lines of many programmes perpetuate racist as well as sexist messages. The forces of evil are always associated with darkness while the forces of good are almost certainly shining and gleaming white. The overall message of such programmes are clear to the many thousands of children that watch them. Goodness and success are embedded within a philosophy that says destroy all that is dark and 'evil' with a mighty male blow or a slash of the sword. Violence is acceptable, as long as the weapon is held by the white hand and if something 'gets in your way, destroy it'. Similarly it is clear that to 'grow up' strong and beautiful you must be white. Society will reward you with success and riches as long as you work hard and recognise 'badness' and destroy it accordingly. The creators of such cartoons obviously dismiss such analysis and, in fact, cover their intentions by implanting 'moral' messages usually at the end of the programme. Despite the subtle 'indoctrination' the message is there for all children. 'White is Right' and Black is most definitely not best.

If we care about out children's emotional and social development under no circumstances should these so called harmless cartoons be allowed to dominate their lives. For the black child the message is again obvious, reinforcing feelings of low self esteem and precipitating identity crisis. For the white child the false idea of racial superiority is bolstered higher and higher. As educators, parents and caring individuals, a complaint must be firmly registered about such programmes.

Such racist and sexist ideologies cannot be allowed to go unnoticed by individuals who are striving towards positive images for all our children. Similarly the programme makers must be made to realize that there are many within our multi-ethnic society that object to such television and will go to some lengths to make their voices heard.

Finally, for those of you have never watched these cartoons, spend an hour viewing such trash. Hopefully you will reach the same conclusion as I have and register your objections accordingly.

Ruth Grindrod

Activities

● Find some books of Skeletor and She-Ra cartoons and the like. Re-write them, if necessary by re-drawing a sample page or two, so as to remove the negative associations attached to black people or women, if you think they are there.

● Research exercise: Do as Ruth Grindrod's last paragraph suggests - watch some of these programmes. Do you agree with her views?

● In pairs: List as many cartoon programmes as you can that you have some knowledge of. Are some worse than others in regard to racism and sexism? Can you establish any general categories or conclusions?

● You might think, having read the article, that some 'heavy thought' has been given to light and juvenile texts. Why bother? Can only 'serious' literature be analysed? Take a favourite childhood story (e.g. from Enid Blyton) and analyse it as Ruth Grindrod has done. Advanced students here might like to attempt this on Tom and Jerry!

● This type of analysis is sometimes given the rather fearful title of 'deconstruction'. You might like to consult a library and/or your teacher for further enlightenment. See, for example, *Enjoying Texts* edited by Mick Burton (Stanley Thornes, 1989) or *Reading Narrative as Literature: Signs of Life* by Andrew Stibbs (Open University Press, 1991).

Looking at Comics

On the next pages you will find two contrasting extracts from comics. We invite you to read them more analytically than perhaps was intended by the writers. What are the unspoken messages in these texts? How far do matters of style, layout, graphics and language combine to reinforce particular messages? Can you find other examples?

© D. C. Thomson & Co. Ltd.

To his Coy Mistress

This poem is written in the form of a monologue but it invites us to see two people present at the scene, he and she (and no one else). This would be persuasion at its most private were we not all invited to become readers of the poem. We become, as readers, the secret onlookers at this moment of intense passion.

Had we but World enough, and Time,
This coyness Lady were no crime.
We would sit down, and think which way
To walk, and pass our long Loves Day.
Thou by the *Indian Ganges* side
Should'st Rubies find: I by the Tide
Of *Humber* would complain. I would
Love you ten years before the Flood:
And you should if you please refuse
Till the Conversion of the *Jews*.
My vegetable Love should grow
Vaster then Empires, and more slow.
An hundred years should go to praise
Thine Eyes, and on thy Forehead Gaze.
Two hundred to adore each Breast:
But thirty thousand to the rest.
An Age at least to every part,
And the last Age should show your Heart.
For Lady you deserve this State;
Nor would I love at lower rate.
   But at my back I alwaies hear
Times winged Charriot hurrying near:
And yonder all before us lye
Desarts of vast Eternity.
Thy Beauty shall no more be found,
Nor, in thy marble Vault, shall sound
My ecchoing Song: then Worms shall try
That long preserv'd Virginity:
And your quaint Honour turn to dust;
And into ashes all my Lust.
The Grave's a fine and private place,
But none I think do there embrace.
   Now therefore, while the youthful hew
Sits on thy skin like morning dew,
And while thy willing Soul transpires
At every pore with instant Fires,
Now let us sport us while we may;

And now, like am'rous birds of prey,
Rather at once our Time devour,
Than languish in his slow-chapt pow'r.
Let us roll all our Strength, and all
Our sweetness, up into one Ball:
And tear our Pleasures with rough strife,
Thorough the Iron gates of Life.
Thus, though we cannot make our Sun
Stand still, yet we will make him run.

Andrew Marvell

Activities

● Is this a good argument? Is Marvell subtle and clever in his persuasion, or just crude? List some ideas in the poem that use sophisticated arguments and some ideas that use crude argument (use the poem's words and phrases). Put them in two columns, and then notice where each comes from in the poem.

● Make a poster of this poem.

● Make a collection of six other love poems or love songs which you feel have something real to say. To what extent is there an argument embedded in them?

LIST OF TEXTS BY THEME

Accent
Steve Bell 'If ...'
Tony Harrison 'Them & [uz]'

Adaptability
Primo Levi 'Weightless'

Animals
Chief Seattle 'The Earth is Precious'
James Thurber 'The Seal who Became Famous'

Architecture
Gavin Stamp 'Leningrad'
Jackie Witkin 'Pictures of Exeter'

Children
Ruth Grindrod 'Children and Cartoons'
Jonathan Swift 'A Modest Proposal'

Colonisation
R. Parthasarathy 'Whoring after English Gods'
Rana Kabbani 'Europe's Myths of the Orient'

The Earth
The Bible 'Genesis'
Chief Seattle 'The Earth is Precious'

Fashion
Fanny Trollope 'Paris and the Parisians'

Films
Groucho Marx 'Running Battle with Warner Brothers'

Governments
Martha Gellhorn 'The Face of War'

Ideology
Ruth Grindrod 'Children and Cartoons'
Paul Theroux 'Being a Man'
Plato 'Expert Opinion'

Images
Edward Said 'Islam and the West'

Ireland
Jonathan Swift 'A Modest Proposal'

Language
Douglas Adams and John Lloyd 'The Meaning of Liff'
Steve Bell 'If ...'

Language (continued)
Clive James 'Freezing Fog Situation'
Ian Oxley 'In a Bar'
The Cox Committee 'Standard English'
Tony Harrison 'Them and [uz]'
Samuel Johnson 'A Journey to the Western Islands'

Law
Charles Dickens 'Bleak House'

Origins
The Bible 'Genesis'

Magic
V. S. Naipaul 'The Crocodiles of Yamoussoukro'

Manhood
Martin Amis 'Paul Theroux's Enthusiasms'
Paul Theroux 'On Being a Man'

Religion
Bulleh Shah 'Neither Hindu nor Muslim'

School
Terry Jones 'Back to School'
Brian Tuffin 'Letter to School'

Seduction
Andrew Marvell 'To his Coy Mistress'

Selling
John Steinbeck 'A Second-hand Car Sale'

Technology
Robert M. Pirsig 'Zen and the Art of Motorcycle Maintenance'

Travel
Clive James 'Falling Towards England'
Samuel Johnson 'A Journey to the Western Islands'
Ian Oxley 'In a Bar'
V.S. Naipaul 'The Crocodiles of Yamoussoukro'

War
Comics 'U.N. Squadron'
Martha Gellhorn 'The Face of War'
Ruth Grindrod 'Children and Cartoons'

Weather
Ian Jack 'Battering and Boiling'

INDEX OF AUTHORS
AND ILLUSTRATORS

ACKNOWLEDGEMENTS

The editors and publishers wish to thank the following who have kindly given permission for the use of copyright material:

Aitken & Stone Ltd. on behalf of V. S. Naipaul for an extract from *Finding the Centre*, published by Andre Deutsch Ltd. 1984 © V. S. Naipaul, and on behalf of Paul Theroux for the article 'Subterranean Gothic' published in *Granta 10*.

Aspect Picture Library Ltd. for the picture 'Legs' by Mike Wells.

Steve Bell for his cartoon 'If....' featured in *The Guardian*, 30 August, 1989.

The Controller of Her Majesty's Stationery Office for an extract from the *National Curriculum: English for Ages 5 to 16* (The Cox Report).

Fleetway Publications for an extract from 'U. N. Squadron in *The New Eagle* comic, 27 October, 1990.

The Folio Society for an extract from *The Trial and Execution of Socrates* by Plato, translated and introduced by Peter George, 1972.

Granta Publications Ltd. for the extract from 'Weightless' by Primo Levi, first published in 'The Story-teller', *Granta 21*, Spring 1987.

Hamish Hamilton Ltd. for an extract from *Sunrise with Seamonsters* by Paul Theroux, and for the illustration and extract from 'The Seal Who Became Famous' from *The Thurber Carnival* by James Thurber.

HarperCollins Publishers for the extract 'The Journey and the Book' from *For Love and Money* by Jonathan Raban, published by Harvill (imprint of HarperCollins Publishers).

William Heinemann Ltd. and Viking Penguin (a division of Penguin Books USA Inc.) for an extract from *The Grapes of Wrath* by John Steinbeck, © 1939, renewed © 1967 by John Steinbeck.

The Independant Newspaper, for the article 'Battering and boiling - This is the Age of the Wind' by Ian Jack, 4 March 1990.

Macmillan Press Ltd. for an extract from *Europe's Myths of the Orient* by Rana Kabbani, and the article 'Whoring After English Gods' by R. Parthasarathy in *Writers in East-West Encounter*, edited by G. Amirthayagam, 1982.

The National Committee on Racism in Children's Books for the extract 'Children and Cartoons' by Ruth Grindrod in *Dragons Teeth*, No 28.

Oxford University Press for the poem 'The Telephone Call' by Fleur Adcock from *The Incident Book*, 1986.

Pan Books Ltd. for an extract from *The Meaning of Liff* by Douglas Adams and John Lloyd, 1983.

Penguin Books Ltd. for the extract 'Back to School' by Terry Jones and a cartoon by Gerald Scarfe from *Attacks of Opinion* by Terry Jones, 1988, and the poem 'Them & [uz]' by Tony Harrison from *Selected Poems* (Viking 1984) © Tony Harrison 1984.

Laurence Pollinger Ltd. on behalf of the Executors and Simon & Shuster Inc for an extract from *The Groucho Letters* published by Michael Joseph Ltd. 1967. Copyright © 1967 by Groucho Marx.

Python Productions Ltd. for an extract from the 'Argument Script' in *Monty Python's Flying Circus - Just the Words* published by Methuen London, 1989.

Random Century Goup on behalf of Robert M. Pirsig for an extract from *Zen and the Art of Motorcycle Maintenance*, published by The Bodley Head, 1974; for an extract from *Moronic Inferno* by Martin Amis, published by Jonathan Cape Ltd., and for extracts by Clive James from *The Crystal Bucket* and *Falling Towards England*, published by Jonathan Cape Ltd.

Routledge, Publishers and Pantheon Books Inc. for an extract from *Covering Islam* by Edward Said, 1981.

Spectator for 'Leningrad' by Gavin Stamp, first published in the *Spectator Magazine*, 16 May, 1981, later in *Views from Abroad: The Spectator Book of Travel-Writing*, edited by P. Smedley and J. Klinka, published by J. Paladin (Division of Collins) 1989.

D. C. Thomson & Co. for an extract from 'Hannah of Horse Heaven' in the *Bunty* comic, 27 October, 1990.

Virago Press Ltd. for an extract from 'Introduction 1986' in *The Face of War* by Martha Gellhorn, 1987.

Every effort has been made to trace all the copyright holders but if any have been inadvertantly overlooked the publishers will be pleased to make the neccessary arrangement at the first opportunity.

Photographic Acknowledgements

The editors and publishers wish to acknowledge, with thanks, the following photographic sources:

G & A Loescher/Barnaby's Picture Library p22, Imperial War Museum p94, Ian Jack/Independant Newspapers p99, Robert Capa/Magnum Distribution p45, National Motor Museum p50, John Sinker p9, Jackie Witkin p19, 20.

The editors would like to thank Joseph Mills and Farman ul-Haq Choudry for their help in providing facilities for researching this volume and for their valuable advice. We should also like to thank our typists, Sarah Evans, Shirley Garbett, Doreen Smith, Kath Smith and Ann Vasilesco.